*God, Miracle and the*
*Church of England*

Bishop Lyttelton
Library

Winchester

Also by David E. Jenkins and published by SCM Press
*The Glory of Man* (The 1966 Bampton Lectures)
*The Contradiction of Christianity*
*What is Man?*

David E. Jenkins
*Bishop of Durham*

# God, Miracle and the Church of England

SCM PRESS LTD

A/44

© David E. Jenkins 1987

*British Library Cataloguing in Publication Data*

Jenkins, David E.
God, miracle and the Church of England.
1. Church of England.
I. Title
283'.42      BX5131.2

ISBN 0–334–02035–2

First published 1987
by SCM Press Ltd
26–30 Tottenham Road, London N1 4BZ

Printed in Great Britain by
Richard Clay Ltd, Bungay, Suffolk

# Contents

# Introduction

I have become engaged in many arguments. From my point of view they all have one theme and one concern. The theme is God. The concern is that I should be part of extending knowledge of God and developing response to God. The arguments are, thus, explorations into God, or arise out of experiences, ideas and questions generated through this exploration by relating something we are allegedly told about God to something going on in the world, or by being compelled by something happening in the world to look again at what we are told, or have come to believe, about God. All this is done from within the Christian church and tradition, since I am a Christian, that is, one who believes that Jesus is a central and decisive clue to the nature, being and reality of God and therefore to the possibilities and promises of the world and of all that goes on in it.

When I became involved in public controversy soon after my appointment as a bishop had been announced, it gradually became clear to me that the theological arguments, that is to say the arguments about what was involved in a Christian faith in God, were not really about miracles, although they focussed publicly on this issue, but were about what sort of God we believe in or should believe in, about what God does, what he wants and what he offers. Hence I have tried to pursue this theme both as part of my own particular discipleship and local ministry and as part of a contribution to the life and mission of the church in relation to society today. I have taken up a variety of invitations for a variety of occasions which have allowed me, or required me, to pursue this theme. I believe that I am developing through them all a coherent and consistent line of exposition and discovery which is certainly helpful to me in the maintenance and development of my own faith and discipleship and which will, I hope, be of assistance to others. Hence my decision that the pieces in this book should be published.

They arose as follows. In 1985 the Board of the Faculty of Theology of Oxford University invited me to give the Hensley Henson Lectures during the academic year 1986–7. I was honoured by this invitation, glad of the opportunity, if I could fit it in, to return to lecture once again at my own university and intrigued and attracted by the opportunity to do something there in the name of a predecessor in the See of Durham for whom I feel a good deal of sympathy and admiration. (Hensley Henson was Bishop of Durham from 1920 to 1939.) Moreover, Bishop Henson in his bequest to the university had laid it down that these lectures should be given by a minister of the Church of England, the Church of Scotland or the Church of Sweden on 'the Appeal to History as an integral part of Christian Apologetics'. If I accepted the invitation I would then be compelled to think further about the ways in which it was proper and possible for Christians to think about and understand God's relation to the goings on of history and to events and activities within the world.

On the one hand this would suggest following up thoughts and explorations about miracles, for they formed a focussing point to do with claims about God's particular acts to be discerned in particular events. On the other hand I saw it as an opportunity to reflect on claims about the church as being something which God somehow developed and authorized in history. It seemed sensible to attempt some reflection on this with particular reference to the Church of England and the Anglican Communion. This would be timely in view of the approaching Lambeth Conference in 1988 but was also directly relevant to current controversies about the authority and identity

viii

of the Church of England in relation to such matters as traditions of belief on the one hand and traditions of order on the other. (This included such subjects as the ordination of women to the priesthood and the discussions of ARCIC about relations between Anglicans and Roman Catholics and such topics as authority and ministry.) Hence I accepted the invitation and offered the title 'Anglicanism, Accident and Providence'. The four lectures I gave in the Examination Schools at Oxford in February and March 1987 form the second half of this book. I had hoped to develop them further, but as they have come out reasonably clearly and do constitute a more or less coherent development, even if only in outline, of a particular line of argument, I decided that they should appear as they were delivered. It is not easy to find time to write and it seems better to make a contribution to an ongoing discussion, rather than wait to complete an argument which can best be furthered in any case in discussion and in decisions. As will be seen, the lectures are deliberately directed both to some questions which are liable to come up at the Lambeth Conference in July and August next year (1988) and to pick up the debate in the Church of England and the Anglican Communion about the ordination of women. The actual lectures were given on both sides of the week in February 1987 when the Synod of the Church of England was meeting in London and included in its agenda a debate on the report from the House of Bishops on 'The Ordination of Women to the Priesthood'. Thus the lectures are an attempt to think systematically and theologically about matters of current debate and concern and to put these matters in the wider context of our beliefs about God, his relation to the world and his dealings with us.

To contribute further to clarifying thought and belief on these issues and to indicate some of the 'working material' which lies behind the arguments outlined in the Hensley Henson Lectures I have put into the first part of the book four occasional pieces of mine delivered between December 1984 and December 1986. The first is my speech to the General Synod of York on Sunday 6 July 1986. This was a contribution to the debate on the Report of the House of Bishops entitled *The Nature of Christian Belief.* The report arose out of a debate in General Synod in February 1985 which itself arose out of the controversies which I, to some extent, had occasioned. It seemed necessary to point out that arguments about details of belief and ways of believing must be considered as reflecting views on, or implicit beliefs about, God and that failure to take this into account could render the debates themselves useless or harmful. I also took the opportunity to relate such debates to the discussions about the ordering of the church. It will be seen that this speech briefly outlines an approach to the identity and nature of the Church of England which is worked out in more detail in the Hensley Henson Lectures.

The second piece was given as a sermon in Hild Bede Chapel in the University of Durham on 6 December 1984 in a sermon series arranged for that term which related Christian faith to various disciplines. I was asked to speak on the discipline of academic theology and took the opportunity to relate this to certain aspects of the basic nature of belief in God.

The other two pieces are directly about miracles. 'A Consideration of Miracles' was a Minster Lecture given at York on 5 December 1986. The invitation to contribute to the York Minster Lecture series seemed an excellent opportunity to reflect as systematically and clearly as possible about the underlying issues which had been exposed by the controversies and discussions so far. Finally, I have added the sermon 'Lord I Believe, Help my Unbelief', which I preached in York Minster on the morning of Sunday 20 July 1986. I preached that sermon because I had been invited to be one of the summer preachers at the Minster and Mark 9.14–29 was the Gospel set for that day. It is appropriate to include it in this book, not only because it attempts to illustrate the practical bearing of the theological reflections about miracles and God's relation to and dealings with us, but also because it illustrates and underlines the point that, for me, there must be a constant interaction between theological reflection, practical preaching and actual dealing with the goings on of the world and the living of our lives.

I offer this small book, therefore, as an interim contribution to practical divinity.

## PART ONE

*God and Miracle*

# 1

## *The Nature of Christian Belief*

As we argue about what is involved in Christian believing and about whether or not women should be ordained to priesthood in the Christian church, there is one question which is more and more forced upon me and which I therefore feel obliged to share with Synod. The question is this. 'Is our God worth believing in?'

Our God, so it is forcefully argued by some, must have performed certified and guaranteed physical miracles in order that the incarnation can have happened and the resurrection be the real and glorious exposition and explosion of divine power that we all believe it to be. He is a God who must have specially and uniquely intervened to transform very particular particles of matter into a particular divine reality, symbol and mystery. This, it is alleged, was necessary so that God could be one with us in and as the human being Jesus, and in order to deliver Jesus fully and personally and finally from the dead. In the case of the incarnation we are concerned with the divine transformation of Mary's chromosomes and genes so that Jesus is a fully human male and, in and as one and the same person, also Emmanuel, God with us. In the case of the resurrection we have the divine transformation of the particular physical make-up of Jesus's corpse so that he is alive, and seen to be alive, in a transformed body which is the necessary sign and symbol of Jesus's being alive in a manner appropriate to glory and to eternity or in a manner preliminary to, and on the way to, glory and eternity.

3

The critical point is the claim that the miraculous and divinely produced transformation must be a directly divinely induced transformation of the physical in order for the incarnation and the resurrection to be believable, real and historical. God's power and presence and commitment must, so it is claimed, in these two particular cases have acted something like a divine laser-beam which fuses the physical particles into a reality which is both divinely produced and divine. It is further claimed that the biblical records both support and require this way of understanding incarnation and resurrection and, even today, allow of no other interpretation and exposition as fully appropriate or faithful.

I wish to set aside all the customary critical and comparative questions which arise and which have to be discussed and lived with concerning the New Testament evidences and their inter-pretation. The question I feel obliged to concentrate on is this. What sort of God are we portraying and believing in if we insist on what I will nickname 'the divine laser-beam' type of miracle as the heart and basis of the incarnation and the resur-rection? I feel obliged to suggest that if we do so insist, then we are implying, if not actually portraying, a God who is at the best a cultic idol and at the worst the very devil. Let me try to explain this deeply troubling possibility.

God, it is apparently alleged, works uniquely and directly in a divine intervention on physical matter in order to bring about his basic saving miracles of incarnation and resurrection. Now please be very clear that it is no part of my argument, exploration and meditation to say that it is clear on theoretical or philosophical or scientific grounds that God cannot do that. God is far too great a mystery, and the created universe, in dependence upon him, is far too open a mystery, for it to be possible for any of us to say what God can or cannot do or what can or cannot happen. Still less am I saying that miracles do not or cannot happen. I am wrestling, in the light of God's unique presence in and as Jesus Christ, with what miracles actually are in a realistic and down-to-earth way.

God, in order to declare and achieve our salvation, chose to become one of us. Jesus was the man God chose to become, and this Jesus, as a man, chose to die in obedience to his Father for the sake of God's kingdom and, as we have come to know, for us women and men and our salvation. This implies and expresses a truly wonderful and utterly gracious identification of God with us. God put himself at our disposal that we might be brought to his disposal. If God is this sort of loving, identifying and gracious God, then surely we must be very careful, reverent and reticent about how we pin certain sorts of miracle on him.

The choice of physical miracles with what might be called laser-beam-like precision and power would not seem to be a choice which he cared, or would care, to use. For if such a physical transformation with precision and power is an option open to God consistent with his purposes of creation, freedom and love, then we are faced with a very terrible dilemma indeed. We are faced with the claim that God is prepared to work knock-down physical miracles in order to let a select number of people into the secret of his incarnation, resurrection and salvation, but he is not prepared to use such methods in order to deliver from Auschwitz, prevent Hiroshima, overcome famine or bring about a bloodless transformation of apartheid. Such a God is surely a cultic idol. That is to say, he is a false and misdeveloped picture of the true and gracious God drawn up by would-be worshippers who have gone dangerously and sadly astray. If such a God is not a cultic idol produced by mistaken and confused worshippers, but actually exists, then he must be the very devil. For he prefers a few selected worshippers to all the sufferers of our world. Such a God is certainly not worth believing in. But I do not believe that we can possibly so have learned Christ.

In fact and in faith, God's relations with the world and with ourselves, including his miracles, are surely something much more mysterious, personal and risky than the knock-down, this-must-be-a-decisive-physical miracle, type of argument and understanding allow. Miracles are most probably something much more historical, real and down-to-earth than

5

monophysitely divine manipulations of the physical. God is much more interwoven with and committed to our flesh and blood, our obedience and collaboration and our freedom and limits. He transforms the natural, not by making it arbitrarily supernatural and so unnatural, but by enabling the unbelievable fullness of what is natural through unity with the unbelievably gracious divine. The birth narratives are far more about the obedience of Mary and Joseph in response to the unique graciousness of God than about Mary's physical virginity. The resurrection narratives are far more about encounters and namings and joyful recognitions than about the empty tomb. Miracles are gifts rather than guarantees, given to faith and perceived by faith, and they always involve a mysterious collaboration and convergence between the intervening power of God and human responses of faith, obedience and activity.

We are always wanting to pin God down by getting things cut and dried and decisive. God is always wanting to set us free to share in the mystery and the suffering of creation, freedom and redemption. God undertook the cross when he undertook creation. We – and especially religious people organized into churches – are always trying to limit the risk, curtail the openness, contract the freedom and avoid that commitment of faith which is the falling into the risk and the abyss of love. I realize that it is stupid and foolish of me to attempt mystical theology in a debate in Synod. But surely we cannot avoid such a folly, for we are debating (must we be debating – could we not be exploring?) faith and the role of women in the church before the mystery of God as this has been declared to us in the face of Jesus Christ.

So to be true and faithful to tradition we must think about the central mysteries of our faith in a way which takes full account of where we now are in our contemporary world. For the central mystery of the incarnation is that God took on the contemporary world. He is not a once-visiting God who froze somewhere between the first and fourth centuries. Tradition is not a noun shaped once and for all in the past; it is a verb active under God now for the sake of the future.

And in so taking on the world, God made it clear that he is not a triumphalistic God who produces knock-down miraculous arguments. He is a being-with and suffering-through God who again and again produces miracles of collaboration and transcendence, all in the midst of our suffering, struggling and oddly glorious world. So the final point of my meditation in mystical theology is this. As he is not a triumphalistic God, he does not have a triumphalistic church.

It simply is not true that there is anywhere a church which is guaranteed to get it right under God. As there are no knock-down miracles which prove to everybody that God is around, so there is no church with knock-down authority which can settle decisively and definitely for ever what God is like and what God wants. To claim this, or to behave as if this were so, is to present an impossible and unworthy picture of God. For if it were the case that there exists a church which is bound to be right when it speaks for God, speaks of God or acts for God, then we should all be bound to be atheists. For the records of all churches contain acts of inhumanity, declarations of stupidity and indications of triumphalism, arrogance and insensitivity which are a disgrace to God – or, indeed to ordinary humanity. It is surely quite clear that it is practically and morally impossible to believe in an ecclesiastical God or a God of the church. God must be far more than, and at times very distanced from, the church or all churches. We worship God, not the church in any shape or form. That was one of the most fundamental reassertions of Protestantism and of the Reformation, and it has to be reasserted again and again. This sort of Protestantism is an essential part of catholic and apostolic faith and practice. Within, under and through this worship of God we thankfully accept that there is a church of God, which he calls, judges, changes and sustains and, above all, mercifully and graciously uses. There is a church of God but there is no God of the church. He is the God of the whole earth and mystery of all things. We belong to him, but he does not belong to us. He identifies himself with us and saves us, but he is sovereign, free, glorious and mysterious.

Two practical postscripts follow, to which I can refer only in a sentence or two, but which deserve our most careful investigation. The first is that it is essential, at any rate for the time being, to preserve the distinctive nature and identity of Anglicanism. We are not papalist Roman and we are not biblicist Protestant. We are clear that all churches err, have erred and will err. We are also clear, however, about the importance of traditional creeds, traditional ministry and being kept together by our worship and our ministry. We rely on God to keep us together, correct us together and move us forward together. For Christian life and witness in the church, belonging is more important than agreeing and it is more important to live, worship and work together than to be in the right. As we live together we shall work out, under God, developing understanding of what is required by our worship of God, Father, Son and Holy Spirit, and of how we embody and express mutually recognized patterns of faith and of baptism, eucharist and received ministry. It is urgently necessary, however, that we remain clear that belonging together is more important than agreeing. God gives himself to us through one another and our differences as much as through Bible or tradition, or a particular way of ordering and practising things. It is the living body which counts. And we need to be clear that living together and serving the world is more important than being right or in the right.

Which leads to the second practical point. We are saved by grace through faith and we have no righteousness of our own. Therefore we are not prevented from being part of the true church, and being fully received by our fellows, by the errors which we make, just as the Church of Rome is not prevented from being part of the true church of God by having made the nearly disastrous error of claiming in 1870 to have an infallible authority. Sin does not have dominion over us. So we are always free to live together, work things out together and to change. We do not have to wait for papal authority to do this. Our concern is not with the past of the Roman church but with the future of the whole church of God. We look, therefore, for the eventual close unity when all have repented and changed.

Therefore we know that whatever our responsibly considered decisions and whatever our worked-out expressions of faith and of order, we are saved by God as much despite them as because of them. We are not able – until the End – to serve God in *his* way. We can serve God only in our respective and imperfect ways which he accepts, blesses, judges, forgives and changes. We need one another, and none of us is in the right.

So we ought to accept the report from the House of Bishops and move on in conversation, commitment, criticism and witness. We need to face the issue of the ordination of women and not be bullied, frightened or dismayed by backward-looking references to tradition or being bound by a past in which God no longer lives. He lives now and for the future. Above all we need to pray very earnestly that God will, of his very great mercy, spare us the ultimate humiliation and horror of discussing him and deciding about the ordering of a part of his church in ways which deny his mystery, his freedom, his infinite openness and his incredibly suffering love.

# 2

## God and the Theologian

### (Fundamentalism fatally flawed)

*For my thoughts are not your thoughts, and your ways are not my ways. This is the very word of the Lord. For as the heavens are higher than the earth, so are my ways higher than your ways, and my thoughts than your thoughts* (Isaiah 55.8–9).

Clearly we cannot define, describe, evaluate or pin down God. This must be so, for God is God; and if he is not beyond us, above us and beyond our grasp, he is simply one of us – one thing among the things with which we can cope – in which case he is not God. As Professor Hodges puts it in his important and exciting book *God Beyond Knowledge*:

> It is agreed doctrine that God is beyond human understanding. This is not merely the hasty reaction of the ordinary man, disheartened at the sight of the problems which arise. It is also the considered judgment of the philosophical theologians who, on grounds of metaphysics and theory of knowledge, work out the doctrine of the Divine Incomprehensibility. (It is not always realized what a strong streak of agnosticism the traditional philosophical theology bears within itself.)

Indeed it is not! So many people are so sure about God that

you can be pretty sure that they know very little about him. But, to return to Professor Hodges:

> And again, when the life of piety develops along the lines which are generally called mystical it arrives by its own road at an apprehension of God as the ultimate Mystery, an apprehension which surprisingly does not at all inhibit the relations of personal intimacy which the contemplative has with his God.[1]

I am sure that this is wholly right, both in logic and in contemplation. In logic, language cannot be adequate for God. He cannot be contained by any of the descriptions which we try to give of him, or by any of the stories which we are authorized to tell of him. Take a miracle. If we know exactly what it is and precisely how it works it ceases to be a miracle, and it cannot be termed a miracle, a wonder speaking of God; without faith a miracle is not perceived as such. Take the resurrection; scan the records in detail and you will find again and again that there is room for doubt, for personal apprehension and, above all, for interpretation. God, when he acts in the salvation of the world, cannot be pinned down and cannot be discerned without a responsive faith.

Take the word 'Father' (a word which has a lot to be said about it yet by the women theologians). If you take it too literally there may be little short of hell to pay. Take the Trinity. It is the most glorious symbol of the ultimate truth which is revealed to Christianity, but if you try and work it out too far you get into a complication which resolves itself either into a celestial tea party or else a cloud with three faces. It will not do! If language cannot contain, then knowledge cannot grasp, and God is always beyond knowledge.

If then we turn to contemplation: I am no great mystic, but I know that when I come near to a contemplative moment it is here that God is experienced to be with me. It is wholly a gift, and never a possession. It cannot be grasped, however much I am grasped by it. When I want God to be near, I must not look towards him or he is gone. Sometimes, indeed, it is an

11

awareness of his absence which tells me that I have known him, assures me that I will know him and therefore gives me an awareness – what shall I call it? – of his presence or his absence which is very real, though it is certainly not graspable, Whatever is known, or given, or glimpsed, it is closer than close, in intimacy and indeed in assurance, but if I seek to grasp it it is gone. It is not be be analysed or examined. God is no object of critical investigation. He is the subject of faith and hope, of obedience, of love and of longing.

How, then, does 'theology' as an academic discipline stand? (I had better establish that if I can, or I have earned my living by pretence for many years.) So how is theology as an academic discipline, as an exercise in analysis which must face with integrity all possible criticisms, practicable, if God is, somehow or other, its 'subject'? How does it stand in relation to Christian faith? Clearly for some there is an apparent clash. I have been the direct subject of this. People have told me that questions which I can ask as a professor I cannot ask as a bishop, or at least I should not ask them openly. Such a suggestion appals me, and in my view comes strikingly close to blasphemy. How dare people suggest that what has to be asked about God cannot be asked in public by an authority of the church? What do they think of the church? Who do they think we are? Who do they think they are? It is appalling, for there seems to be a suggestion that the faith cannot face truth. Surely, theology is something which has to be pursued with the utmost academic vigour and the utmost academic devotion. No questions can be barred. But this is made possible and required by the very giving and the very being of God. It is God himself who compels us to the critical pursuit of truth with integrity and to face every possible question. Of course, I mean the being and the giving of the God who is witnessed by, and who is expressed in, Jesus Christ, and who is experienced at the heart of the Christian tradition.

Christian theology, however, even as an academic discipline, cannot avoid being in some real sense confessional. Theology cannot avoid being confessional, for without the confession of

Jesus as Lord, which expands into the confession and praise of the Holy Trinity, God the Father, God the Son and God the Holy Spirit, there would be no subject-matter for the disciplines that make up academic theology. Let not the students of theology and the professors of theology ever forget this. All the disciplines of Christian theology must take into account that the one necessary strand in the language, the events, the objects and the people they are studying is the strand of confession and praise, of obedience and practice. Therefore theology cannot avoid being in some sense confession. Similarly, Christian theology, even as an academic discipline, cannot avoid retaining or regaining some sense of the contemplative and continuing awareness of God, of the Divine, of the Holy, of the Mysterious. For without at least a claim to such a search or such an awareness, the discipline of Christian theology would have no deposit or subject-matter to study. That is why such a theologian as Anselm (like such a composer as Haydn) could not get down to his work without prayer. Without some imaginative sympathy with the contemplative, no one could expect to appreciate what the deposits of Christian faith, life and church are the deposits of and are the deposits for.

Thus, even as a set of academic disciplines, in a secular university, in a secular world, Christian theology must retain something of the confessional and something of the contemplative. But there is no contradiction between the requirements of this and the requirements of academic integrity and freedom. Quite the contrary. For the God who is confessed is not afraid of facts, and the God who is glimpsed in contemplation is freedom, openness and listening. God is no shadowy illusion, and neither is his world, for he has created it and he has invested his purposes in it. Further, as Christians we are aware that in the pursuit of his purposes he has become one of the created beings in it and poured his spirit into men and women in order to further and consummate his creation, his purposes and his incarnation.

Thus, while there is struggle, and even suffering, both in the practice and in the process of bringing together the confessional, the devotional and the critical, there is no contradiction either basically or in the end between the critical questioning mind and the devout, obedient spirit – no contradiction whatever when all is related to the true God and Father of our Lord Jesus Christ. God demands both, and God requires and offers the consummation of both in an ultimate unity of reality, truth and love, which utterly transcends and wholly fulfils them both.

As St Augustine says at the end of his twenty-two books on the City of God: 'There we shall be still and see; we shall see and we shall trust; we shall love and we shall praise. Behold what will be that end without end, for what is our end but to reach that kingdom that has no end?'[2]

But meanwhile we have to serve the kingdom, to wait for the kingdom and to witness to the kingdom. Until that kingdom comes, and as part of the coming of the kingdom, we have to take absolutely seriously (although not absolutely, for only God is to be taken absolutely, and not even our ideas of God, but only God himself) all that has developed in the history of the world and in the searching of the human spirit. The God whom the prophets of Israel could recognize as active in Cyrus cannot have ceased his prophetic, creative and redemptive activities in history at the end of the biblical era, although some people seem to think that God switched off at approximately AD 90, flashed on round about Luther and has switched off ever since. What sort of God is this who is absent from most of the history of the world? Not the biblical one, not the God and Father of our Lord Jesus Christ.

When the God-given minds of men and women (created in the image of God) develop the explorations, experiments and critical methods of science, of history, of social critiques and psychological investigations they may, of course, put these things to false and dangerous uses, but we cannot doubt that God meant them to be developed, or we are doubting his wisdom, his presence and his power. So we are bound to bring, both to the academic study of theology and to common-sense development of a living Christian faith, all the resources

14

which science, history, sociology and psychology make available to us. Of course, we must seek to use these immense and exciting resources of the critical mind in relation to the worship and humility of the devout and obedient spirit. But in so doing we must be very careful that we do not substitute obscurantism for devotion and claim mysteries where we will not confront muddles. Our God must be the God of truth, and he cannot be served by any pretences whatever. If, in fact, we pretend, in the face, for instance, of careful comparison of the text of the Gospel of Mark with the text of the Gospels of Luke and Matthew that it is still possible to hold that every word of the Bible is directly dictated by God, then we are cheating and so in effect blaspheming against the God who is truth. For such a comparison shows that Luke and Matthew are prepared to exercise free rewriting on Mark. So we must be clear that the Bible is a human book, witnessing to God by the Spirit of God through human means and human errors, as well as human insights. To continue a pretence about some special, magical supernatural guarantee of the very words of the Bible is to deny God in history and reject his use of the human, and to invite the Rationalist Press Association to feel fully justified in regarding all religion as outmoded superstition.

Similarly, the claims of the church and the churches have to be subjected to all the valid insights of a Marx or a Freud or a Durkheim. It is plain as a pikestaff, as Marx said, that religion is again and again used in the interests of the ruling classes (for example, when it is not there is trouble in the *Daily Telegraph*). Freud and his followers and critics have many valid insights, for instance about projection and dependency, which make people want a comforting, father-figure bishop and not a disturbing apostolic one. Durkheim has provocative and revealing questions about the whole business of religion as a social bond so that we are not really concerned about God but about keeping our society and morals together. Ideologies and doctrines of man built up solely on a Marx or a Freud or a Durkheim have, of course, to be persistently and resolutely challenged, but this has to be done with a proper use of, and a proper respect for, what a Marx or a Freud or a Durkheim has brought into our understanding of human history and of our behaviour, corporate and individual. Once a valid question has been raised, there is no going back on it, if you believe in God. There is only going forward from it.

Thus, as God is the God of history and as God has created us in his image, the critical use of all the tools of human reason and study which are required for academic integrity are also required of us for a simple and basic theological reason, the being and giving of God. One of the main contributions, therefore, real faith in God and serious theology ought to make to our present confusions and conflicts is to support us in refusing to accept any orthodoxies, any theologies, any dogmatic acceptance of theories political, economic or psychological which shut up men and women in anything less than God. Theology should be at the heart of all academic integrity and criticism and exploration, because of the being and giving of God.

Let me add to this two footnotes. One, the full use of the critical mind in relation to the devout spirit is required by the very mystery of God – the mystery from which I started. Of course theology, faith and practice at all levels must again and again be criticized by all the resources we have and can use. Otherwise, how do we perceive and challenge the errors, the superstitions and the frequent littleness of actual faith, together with the perpetual tendency of all religious people and all religious systems to be more concerned with my and our religion, its beliefs, its formulae and its practices, rather than with the living God? As one of my numerous correspondents said recently, there is an awful lot of religion about, but very little spirituality. As many people take up religion to hide from God as to get closer to him. More positively, surely we must use all critical resources available to us in order that we may again and again break open our perceived images and practices and beliefs, so that the glory of God may be released, or rather that we may be released on our pilgrimage towards that glory.

Secondly, and finally, it may be said; it is often said: 'But this is impossibly risky.' How can we be sure, if anything and everything can be and sometimes must be criticized? The beginnings of a positive but disturbing answer to this disturbing question lies, I believe, in two further points, the first of which is this. We cannot be sure unless God gives us assurances to which we respond in discipleship and pilgrimage so that we grow in the knowledge of him. Growth in the knowledge of God, as all the saints have known, is growth into the unknown, sometimes through knowing and being known and then into the dark night, and then out again into the light and then through and on again. But we cannot be sure. It is only God who can give us himself. Nothing whatsoever in this world guarantees God; but God gives himself.

The second thing is this – and this may perhaps be in some ways the most difficult thing I have to say, though I come increasingly to think that it is almost the most important. Yes, it is risky, and so is creation. If God had chosen to work by guaranteeing us some certain knowledge, delivered by certain means, which always work, then why does he not work like that in the world at large? But in the world at large, as in ourselves, we are faced with much evil, and much that is wholly and even devastatingly problematical. God must therefore take great risks. Otherwise his permitting, tolerating, taking on board and having to do with evil is intolerable. If God has committed himself to the sort of safe policies of manipulation that some people say he has, then why on earth does he not manipulate for love? Such a God, I believe, is unbelievable in the world. Love has chosen to take much greater risks. The fundamental flaw of any sort of fundamentalism is that it assumes a God who guarantees and controls in detail much more than the world shows that he does.

So a final reason why academic integrity, Christian devotion and Christian theology are wholly compatible is the risky nature of God's whole enterprise. This has the cross at the heart of it for an absolutely basic reason. The cross is the very expression of the reality and the power and the promise of God. So we have to work with him with all the resources we have, and we can do this in hope, despite all the difficulties, all the threats and all the errors, because we believe and are sure that God has committed himself to this risky world. He has been with us as Jesus and he has been crucified for us and he has risen up through risk. The kingdom is not manipulated nor does it come by avoiding risk or by delivering absolute guarantees beyond risk. God calls us in Christ to take on these things, to suffer these things and to live these things for the sake and the certainty of the kingdom. Academic integrity, properly pursued, like life, is full of risks, but we take them because they are responded to, and they can be redeemed by, the grace of God, by the presence of God, and by the promise of God.

# 3

# *A Consideration of Miracles*

The argument of this lecture is that we cannot reflect properly about miracles without reflecting about the nature of God and the manner of his working in the world. Since faith knows that God is mysterious, the manner of his working in the world is surrounded in mystery and miracles are part of that mystery of faith. So 'a consideration of miracles' cannot be anything else than a reflection about God, focussed and given direction by claims, controversies and possibilities clustered around the events, the ideas and the experiences which cause talk of 'miracles'. People who talk about God do tend, from time to time and with some regularity, to talk about miracles. Some people who proclaim themselves believers in God seem to set enormous store by miracles and to hold that miracles are central and critical to faith in God or to the understanding of faith about particularly vital aspects and activities of God. If the Bible is held to be in some way centrally significant to our knowledge of, and to our response to, God, then one strand in the Bible is certainly what we may call 'miracle stories'. So how and why and with what effects do faith in God and talk about miracles go together?

How does one start to answer this question? Although it looks as if raising one more question when one has already raised a sufficient number of sufficiently difficult questions is typical of an academic tendency to escape into questions about questions, or abstractions about abstractions, I am afraid that the need to face the question of one's starting point is a severely practical one. For every starting point has its own perspective and set of presuppositions built into it, and unless one is aware of this and allows for it, one's starting point may wholly determine where one gets to, regardless either of facts or arguments on the way. That is why arguments or statements about miracles can cause so much heat, and both angry and fearful controversies, among those who may claim to be believers in God or to be champions of that belief. For a particular way of understanding, accepting and relying upon miracles can become, consciously or unconsciously, the keystone of a person's or group's edifice of faith. If miracles are questioned – or another way of looking at them is put forward – then it seems as if the whole edifice of faith is falling apart. So the argument is not really about miracles, but about God and about what it is like to believe in him, to be responsive to him, to be on the way of growing into the knowledge of him. Which brings us back to the question of the starting point. If what we are obliged to reflect on is knowing God and responding to him, where do we start – and do we have an agreed starting point – and if so, who are 'we'?

Let us suppose that for the purpose of this consideration of miracles 'we' are Christians or Christian sympathizers and we agree to start from the Bible as throwing light on and as being illuminated by Jesus. I put it this way in order to draw attention to a twofold fact which, as you will see if I succeed in getting my points across, is absolutely central to my consideration of miracles. The twofold fact is this. First, it would not have been possible to recognize Jesus as the Christ of God without the witness to the being, activities and purposes of God contained in what we Christians now call the Old Testament. Secondly, the way we now have to understand and respond to all that is witnessed to and pointed to in the Bible, both Old Testament and New Testament, is to be decisively shaped by the central Christian discovery that Jesus is the Christ of God. Whatever we say, or claim or deduce or imply about God, and about what the Bible helps to put us on to

20

about God, must be consistent with, and decisively checked by, the knowledge that the teaching, suffering and crucified Jesus of Nazareth is the Christ of God. The scriptures point to Jesus as the Christ. So Jesus Christ is the Lord and the key by which we must read, receive and interpret the scriptures.

Thus far I would expect all Christians and Christian sympathizers to be in general agreement with me. From now on I have to describe a journey which, in the first place, has to be my own. I shall seek to describe why I find it to be strongly, even compellingly, in accordance with the demands of Christian discipleship, and I shall try to indicate why I believe all Christians and Christian sympathizers ought to be persuaded of the importance and probably the necessity of following this or a similar course. But I do not claim – or expect – easy or general agreement. I claim only that the points raised and the perspectives suggested require the careful consideration of all who would wish their response to God to be authentically 'in the name of Jesus Christ'. So – a consideration of miracles in the light of the conviction that Jesus is the Christ of God and therefore Jesus is Lord.

In the Old Testament, the God whom we Christians know as the God and Father of our Lord Jesus Christ is clearly portrayed as a God who gets in touch, a God who acts for, through and with his people, a God who has a dynamic purpose, demand and offer. In pursuit of his purposes of holiness, righteousness and steadfast love he clearly intervenes in and through people (he calls and sends prophets and speaks to and through them), and stories are told of his mighty and wonderful works on behalf of his people or as a sign to his people at critical moments. He delivers Israel from the Egyptians through the Red Sea. He helps Elijah to defeat the prophets of Baal. The Latin for 'wonderful works' is *miracula*. The God of the Old Testament, the God of Israel, is, therefore, a God of miracles. These miracles are recorded as signs that God is, and is truly God. We may consider as an example I Kings 18.39, after fire had fallen from heaven to consume Elijah's sacrifice in the face of the impotence of the prophets of Baal: 'and when all the people saw it, they fell on their faces; and they said, The Lord, he is the God'. So 'miracles', as we may call them, serve to keep alive faith in the true God, to evoke obedience from the people of God to be faithful to their calling as God's people and to be signs of the presence of God in their present history and the promise of God for their future. It should be noted that miracles do not, as we might say, 'miraculously transform' the history and nature of the people of God. That goes on in its ups and downs and with all its sins and suffering as well as its celebrations. Miracles keep the life of the people going as a history of God's people and through the awareness of prophets and people of the reality and presence of God. They are signs in the dealings and responses between God and his people.

So it came also to be reported of Jesus of Nazareth, the Jesus who, after his death, was recognized and proclaimed by his disciples as the Christ of God because his resurrection from the dead vindicated his living dedication to, and teaching about, the kingdom of God. His ministry, it was reported, was accompanied by signs and wonders, and when the 'Gospels', presentations of the good news about him as the Christ of God, came to be written, two of them were prefaced with narratives about his birth which contain miraculous events. The stories which reflect the discovery of Jesus's resurrection and its reality by the otherwise disappointed, defeated and despairing disciples likewise contain 'miraculous' elements.

Just as care has to be exercised about how the Old Testament narratives portray the role and effect of miracles, so it has to be noted that the New Testament has, especially in the Gospels themselves, a considerable strand of caution about 'signs and wonders'. Jesus rejects the way of impressing by miracle working in the temptation narratives. (His refusal to contemplate turning stones into bread has to be read along with the narratives of his feeding the multitudes.) Jesus is portrayed as warning, 'Except ye see signs and wonders, ye will not believe' (John 4.48), with which we should compare Mark 8.11f. and parallel passages in Matthew and Luke. In Luke 16.31 (the parable of Dives and Lazarus) Abraham is made to say: 'neither will they be persuaded though one rose from the dead'. At the crucifixion the mockers specifically demand: 'Let Christ the King of Israel descend now from the cross, that we may see and believe.' So the New Testament is not unambiguously for signs and wonders as central to belief in and response to God, and whatever lies within and behind the resurrection stories, it was not something publicly available and overwhelmingly convincing.

Thus there is no doubt that the God who is portrayed in the Bible is the God of miracles. The questions are: 'What sort of God, with what sort of miracles?', and: 'How now should we understand, respond and find the living truth in this portrayal?' Here we come to at least two areas of criticism, controversy and conflict which are, I believe, very widely misunderstood and missed. The first is the question about the relation between modern views of the world and the world-view of the people who were responsible for the actual writings in the Bible. The second, which is related to the first, but needs carefully distinguishing for clarity's sake, is the question of the credibility of those who are responsible for the biblical writings and, especially, the credibility of the authors of the four Gospels. Both these questions are clearly related to a consideration of miracles, but usually get mixed up with such a consideration in confusing and unhelpful ways.

First, the question of how we look at things now and how they looked at things then (the relation between modern views of the world and biblical views of the world). To me it is absolutely spiritually and theologically clear that if you really believe that the God portrayed in the Bible is really the God of the whole of reality, then you must take modern world-views absolutely seriously. It is also clear that taking world-views absolutely seriously is not the same thing as taking any world-view absolutely. (In this an authentically modern and traditional spirituality would converge with much modern philosophical and scientific thinking which is acutely aware of the relative nature of all structures of knowing – but that is a matter to pursue elsewhere and at another time.) To claim that out of faith in the God of the Bible and because of loyalty to his Christ, Jesus our Lord, we must impose on the ways in which we now face up to, reckon with and understand our world and ourselves in it, the patterns and assumptions about the daily and natural world which were those of the author of I Kings or the authors of the Gospels is a simple denial of the God of the Bible. It is a denial also of the biblical insight that men and women, although sinful, are 'in the image of God'.

The God of the Bible emerges as the God of the whole universe who is creator of, involved with, and active through, all nature and all history. Given the expanding universe and the amazing developments of human history and human thinking and exploration it would be wholly unbiblical (that is, entirely inconsistent with the dynamics and nature of the God portrayed in the Bible) to insist that God had, by a particular historically conditioned revelation, dictated, once and for all, a normative world view. Clearly he has not, for he has allowed the world to develop, or collaborated with the world in developing, new things, new events and new understandings. Thus, for instance, to oppose Galileo in the name of faith and the Bible was to combine ungodly manipulation with cowardly lack of faith. And any use of faith, Bible or church to impose what are, falsely, called 'biblical views' on our approach to natural and historical realities remains an ungodly power-seeking and unbiblical lack of faith. The gift of biblical faith in the living God is to enable us to face up to reality as we discover it or it discovers us, not to hide away from it. Thus any consideration of miracles, if it is to be faithfully consistent with the Bible, has to take place within the world as we now understand it and as it now challenges us. The Bible is about how God gets in touch with, challenges and assists men and women for his glory and love and their salvation and fulfilment. Miracles are signs of and part of this mysterious and saving interchange between God and men and women within the world he has made and continues to relate to. They are not strange acts of a foreign God constructing an alien and ghetto-like world over and against the world as it is and as we, in the

24

exercise of our God-given (though humanly abused) powers encounter it and wrestle with it.

Thus to conduct a consideration of miracles in terms of an oversimplified and strictly internal religious controversy between people labelled 'liberals' or 'modernists' (who exclude miracles on the grounds of modern thought in spite of the Bible) and people labelled 'traditionalists' or 'orthodox' (who include miracles on the grounds of biblical pictures in spite of modern thought and the revolution of the last three hundred years or so) is simply a confusing mistake. The God of the Bible is not shut up in the Bible. He is at work in the world, and it is this actual contemporary world, including its self-understandings and achievements and failures, that he is at work in. So the question for all is how he continues now to make himself known and to provide signs of his presence and his being available to men and women. It is not a question of using a biblically-shaped sledge-hammer, wielded by traditional Christians, to punch a hole in closed modern views of the universe so that people who get their faith from the Bible can insist on miracles. It is a question of faithfully, patiently and with spiritual insight, discovering how God weaves himself now into the open fabric of his universe and makes himself known to those whom he particularly calls to serve him in the world and for the world by special gifts and intimations of signs and wonders.

There is no necessary or logical contradiction between taking modern world-views with absolute seriousness and holding that the world, and men and women in the world, in the mystery of creativity and freedom, are open to the mystery, the patience and the passion of God. How this openness works is what we have to find out, just as the Israelites had to find it out on their journeying. They found it out in their world; we have to find it out in our world. Both are God's worlds, and biblical faith assures us that God is active to make himself known in and through both.

This is a fundamental theological and biblical point which is all the more relevant to a consideration of miracles in that it

25

is obvious that claims about miracles and talk about miracles are so rapidly and often caught up into overtones or implications of magic, superstition, manipulation and egocentricity. Miracles are of world-wide provenance and used by all sorts of human and religious enterprises in all sorts of cultures for persuading the gullible, defeating the opponents or impressing and lording it over the faithful. Many claims to be the favoured recipients of miracles are also dangerously egocentric and forms of spiritual self-indulgence, and Christian and biblical consideration of miracles must therefore be very careful to place them and criticize them in a clear context of a careful articulated doctrine of God and a sensitive understanding of Jesus as the Christ of God.

But before I finally come to some considerations on that crucial and central point I must briefly refer to the way in which consideration about miracles gets mixed up with issues about the credibility of the biblical writers and especially of the writers of the Gospels. Here there is still an immense job of patient ground-clearing, teaching and sensitive pastoral caring to be done. It is related to the previous more fundamental point of God's relation to the one world which has within it human beings who are remarkably good at discovery and incredibly ingenious at finding new ways of both seeing things and doing things.

As yet the ordinary life of the ordinary churches has scarcely begun to face up to the simple realities of 'the Bible in the modern world'. People seem unable even to begin to make the imaginative effort which is required to bridge the gap between the first-century honest and committed witnesses who told their stories (and indeed similar honest witnesses in the third century, the fifth century or even the fourteenth century) and honest and committed seekers after truth from the scientific and industrial revolution onwards who are striving to produce accurate and effective historical and scientific reports. It is apparently taken for granted that writers of the New Testament must have supposed that they were giving what *we* call accurate and historical reports when they preached, recollected and wrote down the stories about Jesus. This is quite clearly a simple mistake. Recollected stories (themselves shaped and elaborated through several decades of telling) were set down in absolutely good faith to convey to current hearers and readers the dynamic truths about Jesus and his and our relationship to God. These were and are truths which are the essence of the gospel and the heart of the literally life-and-death matter of the resurrection faith. The truth could be conveyed by telling the same story in different ways, locating it in different places and giving it different details and applications. There is no more reason to suppose that the Gospel stories are any more like newspaper reports or scientific papers than, say, the first life of St Cuthbert was. Authors of deep and passionate faith and commitment to a living realism and truth were witnessing in the manner proper to them and known to their times and their ways to what they knew and believed and were passionately convinced about. So to apply modern critical principles to biblical stories and to find differing layers of historicity, myth, legend and sheer embroidery is in no way to call in question either the total good faith and credibility of the writers or the validity and authenticity of their witness. They are simply doing it in their way – which is the way God always works through. Now we have to rely on the same God to make the witness, the truth and life-and-death matters of salvation powerful in our day and our way.

It is clear, as I say, that at the moment the church and the churches cannot become publicly, simply and peacefully adapted to a working recognition of this, but it is necessary to state it clearly and forcefully in a consideration of miracles. Otherwise the consideration is constantly confused by a mis-placed argument of the sort: 'But you must believe in miracles like this which happen in this particular way because otherwise you are making Gospel writers liars or cheats or dupes.' This type of argument is wholly without weight and carries any force it has from a psychological problem about appreciating and appropriating the differences between thinking and feeling about truth and the world (and indeed ourselves) before the scientific and industrial revolutions and after them. The vital point is that the God in whom we believe is one and the same God throughout and it is *now* that we have to seek to perceive his presence and his signs in the terms and conditions which he allows us to live in. We cannot be transported back in a biblical escape machine and it is a denial of the God of the Bible to want this. He is always the contemporary God who is working for the future. *That* is the biblical God.

Thus a consideration of miracles requires us to ask how we can expect to find signs and wonders now within the mystery of God's dealing with the world which remains his world and remains the world within which he is active to be in touch and to save. This is where faith in Jesus as the Christ of God bears most directly on a consideration of, and even a discovery of, miracles. The crucial point is this: How does God exercise his power, reveal his presence, establish his possibilities and promises? It seems too often to be assumed that because, if he is God, he is 'God Almighty', he must do this, at least on significant occasions, in what I have come to call 'knock-down ways'. The basic picture, implied or explicit, is of God the Almighty King – and, since Constantine, of God the Almighty Emperor. And the point about such a cosmic king or emperor is that he is all-mighty, and being all-mighty means being wholly irresistible in a knock-down, take it or leave it, irresistible way. A miracle is then thought of as, so to speak, a localized and controlled explosion of that sort of power. This is God being irresistibly God and making clear that he is irrefutably God. Along this way of thinking miracle becomes, or can become, the principal evidence that God exists and that he is God. Look – *God* did that – it is a great and mighty wonder (even in a strictly localized and limited case) – it is too wonderful to have been done by any other power – therefore God did it – which proves to all that have eyes to see that God is – and indeed is God. But, if we really and truly take with utter seriousness the Christian symbol and doctrine of the Trinity, is this line of thinking properly open to us?

Let us suppose we believe – as I do – that Jesus of Nazareth is the Christ of God and therefore rightly recognized and proclaimed by the church as 'of one substance with the Father', as the Creed of Nicaea declares. This means that Jesus of Nazareth is God in the same sense as God the Father is God. (To be 'of one substance with the Father' is to be God as only God can be God – i.e. in the same sense as God [the Father] is God and not in some derived, lesser or merely symbolic sense.) What does this say about the exercise of God's all-mightiness in the world, through the world and for the world? Surely it says that God is not an Imperial Caesar God of knock-down power but a creative servant God of invincible love. Because we fear freedom, are not yet ready for the totally mutual interdependence of love and do not yet have enough faith to be other than appalled at the risky nature of freely creating love and the alarmingly fragile, although amazingly existing, universe that this has allowed to come into being, we tend to want a God who is in control after the fashion of Caesar, so we construct religions which do exactly what Freud, Marx and Durkheim say they do – meet our psychological needs, support our vested interests and provide bonds for our highly imperfect societies. We do not have a God who is in control after the fashion of Caesar. We have a God who is creating control after the fashion of Christ. At least, so it seems to me if one is really trying to be a disciple of Jesus Christ.

The miracles, the communicating and encouraging signs and wonders which are the authentic miracles of this God and of his Christ will not therefore be any or every member of the class of mystifying and wonder-making events which occur across the world for all sorts of reasons, objective and subjective, known and unknown. They will be those combinations of events, personal perceptions of events and presence of God which evoke that response of faith which is appropriate to the God and Father of our Lord Jesus Christ. This God has shown himself in Jesus, through Jesus and as Jesus, to be the creative power of holy, righteous and steadfast love committed to working through the world and to bringing out of the world the fulfilment of the sharing of his creativity and love. Miracles are part of encountering the openness and presence of God within the textures, structures and activities of the created world. They are produced and experienced by means of the space which is kept open, or made open, in that world by the intercourse of God with free and searching persons. This is why an authentic and genuinely revelatory miracle is always a mysterious combination of active and experiencing faith along with a sense of, and conviction about, a gift which goes beyond the ordinary, while experienced in and through the ordinary. There is always a way of interpreting or explaining a 'miracle' which does not oblige anyone to attribute it to God. To put it another way, miracles can be perceived and identified only by personal faith within the tradition, story and community of faith. But this does not mean that miracles are only subjective experiences. It means that God does not force himself on people. He offers himself to us for our response, obedience and collaboration.

I would like to try to illustrate what is behind this point by asking you to join in what is sometimes called a thought experiment. Let us suppose that the experiments which, it is reported, are currently being conducted on the Turin Shroud were held to produce scientifically compelling evidence that it was (a) of the right period to be co-incident with the burial of Jesus and (b) that it had wrapped a body which both bore marks appropriate to the crucified Jesus (thorns penetrating the head, nail marks, wound in the side and so on) and was a body which had been, let us say, 'photo-dynamically' transformed. Let us waive likely difficulties about the effective limits of error in radio-carbon dating and difficulties about the history and transmission of the piece of cloth and make an 'ideal' thought-experiment of granting my initial suppositions. That would mean that we are assuming that the evidence produced was such that it was sufficiently widely agreed across the community of communities that make up the scientific community that the date of the Shroud and the 'photo-dynamism' of an identifiable body had been established. Do you suppose that then the resurrection stories of the Gospel would be seen to be *proved* in such a way that millions of people would then become Christians? That is to say, would be convinced of the reality, love and availability of the God and Father of our Lord Jesus Christ and see that the thing they most wanted to do was to throw in their lot with all the other Christians and make the responding to God and the following of Jesus Christ the basis, the content and the aim of their lives?

Surely the answer to the basic question of the thought-experiment, i.e., 'If this were proved, would people be compelled to living faith in and commitment to the God and Father of our Lord Jesus Christ?' is 'No.' All that would happen would be that some rather doubtful and disturbed Christians would feel confirmed both in their faith and in the particular way they held it and a few waverers of a certain sort might be persuaded to think again. But the compulsion of love and faith to commit oneself to the presence and the possibility of God would not arise out of such an exercise. It would not arise, first because people are not put on to God by exterior evidences but by internal and shared experiences. And it would not arise in the second and more basically important place because it is clear from the life and story of Jesus Christ that God does not work like that. Miracles do both evoke faith and indicate faith and develop faith, but they do not compel faith and certainly do not compel faith in public and external ways. Miracles are *gifts* – to faith and for faith, but not public and objective pressures into faith. They are not so because God is not like that and faith is not like that. The mockers of Jesus on the cross got it precisely right. The kingdom and lordship of God is not manifested by public acts of spectacular power. There was no 'coming down from the cross' that everyone might believe (might believe what – that God was the tyrant of tyrants and emperor of emperors?). The miracle of God's love, of Jesus's obedience, and of our salvation lay through desolation and desertion and death and in the miracles of resurrection faith and all that follows and continues to follow from this and as this. It simply is not the case, either in the biblical records or through the subsequent history of the world

31

and of the church, that the God and Father of our Lord Jesus Christ works manipulative and compelling miracles. This remains true and has to be reasserted as true, whatever Christians and the Christian church have been wont to say. The church and Christians are always falling for the mirage of the emperor God when Jesus is Lord and Saviour on behalf of the servant God. Miracles always have been and always will be the wonders of personal love mysteriously woven into the open fabric of the universe through the acts of God collaborating with the response of obedient and faithful persons, persons often surprised into, or caught out by, their obedience and their faith, so that all is gift and grace but nonetheless never nothing but the compulsion of an imperial and imperious God.

All this, of course, leaves practically everything about miracles to be discussed, but I am not going to go on any further. I hope I have sufficiently shown why mere to-and-fo controversy about miracles, or about this miracle or that, is both useless and faithless. We have to get behind the controversies to a careful, patient, open and humble exploration and discovery about the reality of encounter with the God and Father of our Lord Jesus Christ in and through the realities of our time.

For my part, I am quite clear that miracles occur. I am clear about this because I am part of the community who believes in God through Jesus Christ and because of my personal experience, conviction and commitment. But I am equally clear that I do not believe in God nor in his Son Jesus Christ our Lord because of miracles. Because God is there and because God is active and God is loving, and because I and all my fellow human beings are potentially open and free beings in the image of God, there is no telling what wonderful signs, intimations and gifts are to be received in the gracious and mysterious dealings between God and men and women in his world. But one thing is clear. God will not deny himself as he has shown himself to be in Jesus Christ. We may be sure therefore that miracles are not proofs of power but gifts of love to be received by faith. Further, they are to be responded to in life and by praising and by trusting God, whether he gives us more miracles or whether he does not.

32

# 4

## Lord I Believe! Help my Unbelief

*When Jesus, with Peter, James, and John, came back to the disciples they saw a large crowd surrounding them and lawyers arguing with them. As soon as they saw Jesus the whole crowd were overcome with awe, and they ran forward to welcome him. He asked then, 'What is this argument about?' A man in the crowd spoke up: 'Master, I brought my son to you. He is possessed by a spirit which makes him speechless. Whenever it attacks him, it dashes him to the ground, and he foams at the mouth, grinds his teeth, and goes rigid. I asked your disciples to cast it out, but they failed.' Jesus answered: 'What an unbelieving and perverse generation! How long shall I be with you? How long must I endure you? Bring him to me.' So they brought the boy to him; and as soon as the spirit saw him it threw the boy into convulsions, and he fell on the ground and rolled about foaming at the mouth. Jesus asked his father, 'How long has he been like this?' 'From childhood,' he replied; 'often it has tried to make an end of him by throwing him into the fire or into water. But if it is at all possible for you, take pity upon us and help us.' 'If it is possible!', said Jesus. 'Everything is possible to one who has faith.' 'I have faith,' cried the boy's father, 'help me where faith falls short.' Jesus saw then that the crowd was closing in upon them, so he rebuked the unclean spirit. 'Deaf and dumb spirit,' he said, 'I command you, come out of him and never go back!' After crying aloud and racking him fiercely, it came out, and the boy looked like a corpse; in fact, many said, 'He is dead.' But Jesus took his hand and raised him to his feet, and he stood up.*

*Then Jesus went indoors, and his disciples asked him privately, 'Why could not we cast it out?' He said, 'There is no means of casting out this sort but prayer'* (Mark 9.14–29).

Our Gospel today tells a story of Jesus healing an epileptic boy. He does this after his disciples, in his absence, had been unable to do so. Now what is the point and the force of that story for us here and now? All of us have probably been troubled at one time or another by the mystery and the threat of irrational and self-destructive human behaviour in acute forms. Some of us, I guess, have been very closely and nearly troubled by this sort of thing in people near and dear to us. Epilepsy, especially in its more acute forms, is very distressing. But at least it has become recognized as a malfunctioning of the brain and the nervous system which can to a considerable extent be modified by treatment. We do not now commonly and instinctively understand epileptic attacks as manifestations of possession by an evil spirit. But schizophrenia, and other psychotic conditions, are even more haunting and daunting. People disappear into a world of their own and live totally private lives, often agonized, which cut them off from communication with other people and shut them up with experiences of isolation, fear, fantasy which have no traceable connection with what we normally regard as the common and shareable world. Here there is no commonly agreed, and obviously convincing, explanation, of the causes and of generally available and readily successful ways of dealing with many of the cases.

So, if we dare to hope that people are made by love for love, how should we face up to this terrible malfunction and misery and unapproachable alienation?

For example, does the detailed and moving story we have just heard from St Mark's Gospel mean that the New Testament is telling us, on divine and revelatory authority, that the reason for these threatening invasions or distortions of being a person or a self is possession, possession by evil spirits, and that the cure of these wretched conditions for women and men and children is something called faith, if only we had it and exercised it in the right way?

Recall the story. The boy's father says, 'But if it is at all possible for you, take pity upon us and help us.' 'If it is possible!', said Jesus. 'Everything is possible to one who has faith.' 'I have faith,' cried the boy's father, 'help me where faith falls short.'

Now that is one of the examples, I am afraid, where the New English Bible translation tries to smooth over paradoxes in the Greek. The trouble with moderns is that we keep trying to want to explain things instead of living with the mystery. What the Greek actually says is that the father bursts out and cries, 'I believe! Help my unbelief.'

The father's faith was not falling short. He had faith because he had glimpsed something in Jesus which he longed for for his child. But he did not have faith because he did not dare. It was too much to hope for. 'Lord, I believe. Help thou my unbelief.' No falling short. Surely that is much more like what true faith is, really. Risky commitment to a glimpsed possibility in the face of reasonable human hesitation about whether it is really possible.

Talk about faith falling short rather reminds one, I fear, of those somewhat alarming sects or individuals who seem to want, so to speak, to blackmail you into hyping up your faith on the grounds that, if you jack it up, the faith pressures will somehow compel God into a miracle. Here faith comes dangerously close to being an attempt to manipulate God.

But real faith is surely something very different, the sort of thing you have and do not have, and that is why you go on having it. Afterwards the disciples asked him privately, 'Why could not we cast it out?', and he said, 'There is no means of casting out this sort but prayer.'

Whatever is behind the story, and whatever the story means, it is not simply about some human, psychological pressure or process called faith triggering off wonder-working cures from God. But we certainly do have a resonating and vivid story with a very human realistic note about it.

Is the story therefore really an invitation and a challenge to us to get down to curing, say, epilepsy or schizophrenia by faith? That is, by simply believing that God can cast out, and himself wants to cast out the evil spirit or disentangle the psychotic complex or reorder the disordered neurophysiology? And if we simply believe that God can do this and so ask him to do it, then will he do it?

You will already, perhaps, have guessed that my faithful reflection and my theological judgment tells me this is not so, or certainly not normally so. The Gospel story is not operating, nor meant to be operating, as a historically or scientifically descriptive picture of a divine, or a divinely inspired, diagnosis and cure of epilepsy. And the issue of faith is something far broader, deeper, more open and more risky than whether or not we can bring ourselves to believe that God does a particular thing, in a particular way, so that we are bound and obliged to recognize it as a miracle.

First of all, what is the status of the Gospel story presenting this incident? It is one of a series of such stories to be found in a book which begins like this: 'Here begins the Gospel of Jesus Christ, the Son of God.' That is the first verse of the first chapter of Mark, and the Gospel of Mark is itself one of four such books, the last of which has this at the end of its last chapter but one: 'There were indeed many other signs that Jesus performed in the presence of his disciples which are not written in this book. These here written have been recorded in order that you may hold the faith that Jesus is the Christ, the Son of God, and that through this faith you may possess life in his name.' (That is what we call the thirtieth and thirty-first verse of the twentieth chapter of the Gospel of John.)

That is to say, Gospel stories are written down to announce a faith in Jesus as God's Christ and God's Son and to share that faith by provoking like faith, and sustaining similar faith. The stories are products of faith and preaching of faith. And over the past hundred years or more, a vast amount of faithful, careful and comparative studies of the actual texts of the Gospels, both within themselves and compared with one another, have shown beyond all reasonable doubt that the faithful, believing and trustworthy writers of these Gospel documents simply did not share our concern for our types of either historical or scientific statements. They could not – nobody had thought that sort of thing up.

They believed in Jesus as the Christ and the Son of God. They picked up the stories of belief and faith that were around in the living and believing church, and they wrote them down by writing them up. They wrote them up so that they would reflect their faith and share their faith. Their world was not our world, so their way of understanding the epilepsy need be nothing like ours. What we are invited to share and have the opportunity to share – and indeed the challenge to share – is their faith. And I am preaching to you here in this Christian pulpit and on this Gospel text precisely because I share not only their faith but also their burning and urgent desire that other people should see and hear the bearing and content of this faith – this faith in Jesus as the Son and Christ of God – and come themselves to share it deeply and praise God persistently and appropriately.

The story, therefore, is not important for its historic, still less for its scientific, descriptive accuracy. It is important for its message. As I have tried briefly to show by my comments earlier on the text of the story itself, the narrative resonates with human authenticity. I myself am personally convinced that there was some real, actual, particular incident behind it out of which the detailed story grew. I am also wholly convinced that this story, like all the other Gospel stories, reflects and mirrors – although in culturally limited and inevitably partial ways – the actual impact of the particular and historical man Jesus on those who encountered him, and especially on those who became his disciples. Something very remarkable was going on here, and being built up here, and there: here and there through the living and teaching and acting of Jesus of Nazareth. The question is, what was going on and building up?

This is where, with this particular story, I personally come back to the question I raised earlier, partly because I hover on the edge of the activities of a number of friends in the medical profession, not least the psychiatrists. Where we are faced with personal disorders, like acute epilepsy or apparently intractable schizophrenia, if we may dare to hope – and if we are Christians we certainly may dare to hope – that people are made by love for love, how do we face up to this terrible malfunctioning and misery and unapproachable alienation?

The story is bearing witness to, and inviting us to share in, a down-to-earth and practical faith in a present wrestling and promising God who does not give us any easy answers to the problems, threats and mysteries of destructive and random evil, but who is with us and available to us: with us and available to us both in enduring those evils and in overcoming them.

Jesus made his impact as being intimately in touch with and in some way actually and powerfully expressive of a power and a love of God which has the capacity to overcome the inexplicable, the irrational and the destructive and to restore people to living and creative relationships. In other words, there is a God who has, and who is building, a kingdom of love, and he is always with us, and always for us, in moving towards that kingdom, or in endurance on our way to that kingdom. Miracle stories are signs of this picked up by faith and conveyed by faith to faith. Miracles are not manipulatory, or manipulated, events which can be produced in a routine way by forms of faith or prayer, as if they were God's basic way of dealing with evil and establishing his kingdom. Look at the world. Look at Jesus. They are signs of faith to faith for faith. Faith that God is; that he is building his kingdom and that he is with us and for us to that end, in just the sort of world in which we find ourselves living, and where we still cannot cope with schizophrenia.

So, with regard to epilepsy and schizophrenia and much else, this means we are set free – and indeed urged – to do two things. First, to do all that we can to search out the scientific, physical, psychological and social causes of disorders like epilepsy and schizophrenia, and to seek hopefully for cures, mitigations and renewals. We are fellow workers with God, who is as he is in Jesus – striving and suffering to order and re-order disorder, all in the interests of persons and love.

And secondly, we are free to endure and be supported in suffering, confusion, and a sort of unknowing bafflement – all hopefully. Alongside the shattering experience of having one we love and know shut up, seemingly incurably, in utter madness and misery, we are to set the knowledge of faith, the faith that God, especially focussed in Jesus, has given us sufficient signs of his presence with us, of his suffering in us, and of his living and loving for us. So we continue in faith and hope and love. But the basic practical sustenance of it all is not miracles but prayer.

His disciples asked him privately, 'Why could we not cast it out?' He said, 'There are no means of casting out this sort but prayer.' Miracles may from time to time come as signs of God's love, God's kingdom and God's availability. But the regular way of the kingdom is the regular way of the life of Jesus, a way open in prayer to the diseases and disorders of the world, to the needs and the relationships of men and women, and to the glory, the compassion and the presence of God.

## PART TWO

# Anglicanism, Accident and Providence

# 1

## *What is Church History?*

I accepted the invitation to give these Hensley Henson lectures as an opportunity to put some analysis and reflection together so that I could address a pressing, practical problem in practical theology. The problem is certainly pressing in one precise form for a bishop in the Church of England and the Anglican Communion, but it is a problem exemplifying a much wider set of theological questions of clearly general interest. The problem fits bang in the middle of the subject matter which is laid down as the necessary topic of these lectures: the appeal to history as an integral part of Christian apologetics. It is doubtless an accident of history, or a coincidence, that I should be pursuing this problem in the week before, and in the week after, the General Synod of the Church of England which is considering a report from the bishops about the ordination of women to the priesthood which is quite clearly raising this problem in a sharp form both practically and politically. I leave it to you, therefore, to conclude for yourselves (independently of the obfuscations which I shall introduce into the argument during these lectures) whether I am doing that by chance or by providence.

The problem was, and is, the appeal made to history by people on various sides of debates in which the churches – and in particular the Church of England – are currently involved. It is a problem which is related further to the identity of the Church of England and of Anglicans in relation to the church at large, and to Christianity at large. I mean, of course, questions like the ordination of women, which is now forcing a critical problem on the Church of England: Who do we think we are, and how do we decide who we are? And I mean the discussions of the Anglican and Roman Catholic International Commission and the questions which are around, about which reams of paper are already circulating through the world, about what is the Anglican Communion. (The sub-title of that is *Shades of Lambeth '88*.)

So, the general area of theological interest comes down in a particular way. In what way, or ways, should what has happened in history be taken as significant for Christian believers in God, especially as they are concerned with the ordering and directing of the church? How does our answer to that problem affect our understanding (those of us whom it concerns) about what it is to be Anglicans? Of course, any question about the bearing of what has happened in history immediately raises the question 'And who decides what has happened in history and how do they do it?' Which is why I have entitled my first lecture 'What is Church History?' Being a philosopher I do not, of course, intend to answer that question, and it is clear that each one of my lectures ought to be a series in itself. But it is surely necessary, both at the theoretical level and at the practical level, to review all these things together from time to time if we are to get any theological perspective or grip on what is going on now. I sometimes have the unworthy reflection when I am concerned with debates in the General Synod of the Church of England that these debates are very often taken up by people being sure about things which we cannot be sure about in order to make claims about questions which are of singularly little importance so we can avoid facing up to questions of first-class importance. This is no doubt an unworthy thought, but it is one which is reinforced in me again and again. Therefore, risks have to be taken by someone in trying to put together, in some sort of perspective and some sort of conspectus, what is the worth of these arguments, the weight of these arguments, about which people are getting so

44

singularly worked up. My problematic, as you might say, can perhaps be illustrated by two instances, the first a major one from the fifth century and the second a minor one from today.

The major one from the fifth century is one which I particularly cherish because once upon a time I used to lecture on christology from its origins to Chalcedon in the Oxford Schools. In his history of the Council of Chalcedon, R. V. Sellers writes at a certain point when discussing the run-up to the Council of Chalcedon:

> These letters – [letters from Rome to Constantinople] – (dated 16 July 450) the delegates took with them to the Capital. What the outcome would have been had not the Emperor Theodosius fallen from his horse, and died on 28 July, we can only conjecture. Assuming that each side had remained adamant, East and West, it is reasonable to suppose, would have gone their separate ways – the East, upholding what had been determined at Nicaea and confirmed at Ephesus, and speaking of the 'one nature' (= one Person) of Jesus Christ, the West continuing to preserve its traditional doctrine, first defined by Tertullian, that Jesus Christ is one Person, and that in him are the two natures of Godhead and manhood. But the unexpected happened, and the history of Christian doctrine followed a course which at that time none could have anticipated.[1]

That is in the middle of a serious, if somewhat dull and lengthy, study of church history. The learned scholar Aloys Grillmeier puts it somewhat differently but quite interestingly in his *Christ in Christian Tradition*:

> On 16 July 450, Leo sent a Roman delegation to the East to give events a new turn by direct negotiations. – [There we have, of course, human intentionality.] – To this delegation Leo again gave his *Tomus ad Flavianum*, this time with an anthology of extracts from the Fathers and his Epistles 69– 71. The expected change came, however, not through the efforts of the delegation but with the sudden death of the

Emperor Theodosius (28 July 450) and the accession of the Empress Pulcheria. The delegation was immediately able to reap the fruits of the new situation, as the Tome of Leo was now received with great reverence and carefully translated into Greek along with the extracts of the Fathers. In this form it was promulgated at a synod of Constantinople in October 450. One of the first measures of the new Empress was the deposition of Eutyches' protector, the intriguer Chrysaphius. With this the fate of Eutyches and of the synod of 449 was sealed. On 25 August, Pulcheria took as her consort and co-regent a vigorous and capable officer, the Thracian Marcian. Even in the notice of his election to Leo, the new Emperor expressed his readiness to join with the Pope in restoring the shattered peace of the church by a new General Council. In Marcian, who both spoke and thought in Latin – [Thank God we have got away from these wily Greeks!] – and in Pulcheria, Leo found the help necessary for ordering the church of the empire and clarifying christological belief.[2]

You will notice the tendency in the presentation. Now – to put matters in a very crude way – in order to produce Chalcedonian orthodoxy did God push Theodosius off his horse? Or conversely (this is a different formulation of the same problem, possibly a better one), since a major historical cause of the turn of events leading up to Chalcedon was the accidental death of the Emperor Theodosius, what godly authority can the Council's decisions have?

These, no doubt, are too crude as formulations, but there are times when it would seem necessary to come as clean as possible about these things in view of the weight given by some apologists to historical points which are said to justify – if I may pick a word out of the air – schism. Or, as these are Hensley Henson lectures, what is a legitimate apologetic appeal to history? All the more so – and all the more apposite for Anglicans and members of the Church of England in view of the various accounts of the role of Henry VIII – in what, for the moment, I will call the break with Rome; or however the emergence of the Church of England, in some sense, over and against Rome, in the sixteenth century, is to be described. Hence the title of my second lecture: 'Historicism and Acts of God'. Do we rightly spot God directly, deliberately promoting certain trends or turns in history?

To pin all this to things as they are actually going on, perhaps I may be allowed to interpolate the second example, which is of an autobiographical nature: last night, when I was performing my duties as bishop and instituting someone to a living just south of the Tyne, I read out the customary document. And the customary document begins: 'David Edward, by Divine Providence Lord Bishop of Durham'. I should add that owing to certain historical accidents, unlike the bishops who are my junior, with the exception of the Bishop of Winchester, I am by divine providence and not merely by divine permission! (The permission comes from 10 Downing Street!) Now we do well to laugh, and I certainly do not regard this as a licence to believe that everything I say or do, after due reflection and prayer, is guaranteed by God. But am I to take it as a cross between a mediaeval hangover and a contemporary joke, or what? The Bishopric of Durham has, in some visible ways, amazing continuity. Durham Cathedral has in it the tombs of Cuthbert and Bede; there are lists on the cathedral wall which go back to the tenth century and into which my name has now been chipped. Auckland Castle, in which we live (thanks greatly to the efficiency of my wife) was built from the twelfth century onwards. There is continuity, certainly? Is there identity?

What sort of identity? And what is the significance of whatever identity there is? And how am I implicated in this before God and man? As you might put it – what weight does it have? For what, with whom? Is there a prescriptive element in the weight it should have, or is it just a descriptive element? Such as, for instance, owing to what you might call the sociologically backward nature of the parts in which I live, the Bishop of Durham is regarded by people north of the Tyne, and no longer in his diocese, as well as south of the Tyne, as a person of importance whose attendance at anything is thought to be, if not a blessing, at least some sort of cachet, and who is expected to represent the county wherever he can get to. But that is a simple description of a sociological survival, is it not?

The problematic is clear enough. Can church history help? Can those who write church history give us guidance? Here, of course, I had better remind myself and you of the elementary but tricky ambiguity of a phrase like 'church history', the two sides of it: what happened here and there in and in connection with the church, and the genre of writings about these happenings.

When we come to the genre of the writing of church history – and here I shall be grossly oversimplifying for the sake of making a point, but will be making a point about the way people use history to make points – it seems to me, quite soberly and seriously, that of course we have to reckon with the fact that all church history is propaganda. Of course, all history is written from a point of view. That, I believe, is now fairly universally agreed and a historiographical commonplace. Any historian has to decide what interests her or him and why. This, however, does not mean that historians can write history as they like. There are the canons of the trade, the disciplines of the craft and the criteria about evidence, sources and critical method which have to be discussed and assessed in public discourse with peers among historians at large.

Even here there are problems both within and from Marxist historians, at least those of them who continue not just to be influenced by Marxism as an illuminating way of seeing many historical problems and series of events, but who hold that Marxism provides a decisive set of models for perceiving what is really going on. True believers also challenge the non-Marxist historians with having a built-in failure to see and interpret what is really going on. But this is clearly a problem about historiography and in history and the study of history which is exactly analogous to a Christian-inspired claim to interpret history perhaps, as one might say, providentially – at least providentially in the strong sense of claiming that you need to be let in by revelation on the divine secrets in order to be able to perceive and respond authentically to what is really going on.

Now I am clear that such a claim, whether it comes from Marxists or Christians, is rightly characterized as historicism and is false. The decisive detection and refutation of historicism is, of course, Sir Karl Popper's classic *The Poverty of Historicism*. I shall therefore touch on this matter in my next lecture and meanwhile continue with my observations about church history as propaganda.

By church history I mean that discipline and genre which is generally included among the subjects studied in theology faculties and includes those books which are usually written by church historians – i.e. those who, from some basis of commitment within some church or other or else now, some of them, in reaction to such a basis of commitment at one time, concentrate on teaching, research and the writing of church history focussed on the various aspects and developments of Christianity as focussed in its institutions.

The concern of church history can be characterized as the various manifestations and activities of Christians, especially as organized in churches outwards, so to speak. Church history is not a matter of concern first with secular history or with general history, manifested, perhaps, in paying attention to religious aspects. That is something else. Nor is it secular history, whether written by Christians or others, which happens to have, say, a good deal to do with the Christian church, because the Christian church is being written about in periods when that church was politically and culturally important or even dominant. By church history, I mean history written from a point of view within the churches (or consciously over and against it) and written about the church and the churches, however much the history, as it were, spills over into history at large.

This is the sort of church history to which proponents of various views in current church controversies appeal, and which they cite as a source of authority – or at least as a source of criteria for judgments about what the church should do today: how it should be ordered today and how we may regard its standing, even before God, and certainly in the world today.

Now it surely is clear that all such church history is propaganda and bound to be. Bound to be because the very existence of the church, with its Bible and its traditions, makes some sort of claim about God, the world, the way things are, the way things will be, and the way things ought to be. Hence, anyone writing from within a positive, or directly opposed, approach to the church and to church history is bound to be responding to some problem or other in the light of the church and to be producing some case or other in relation to this problem. I might add that in this set of lectures, as is already clear, I am certainly doing this. I don't think I am writing church history; I think I am trying to reflect theologically and empirically about the church in history – but I am certainly making a case. So let it not be supposed that I am telling people off for making a case. If I am, I am simply demonstrating solidarity in sin. It is, I think in fact, no use complaining about this, but it is necessary to draw attention to it because it raises far-reaching questions about the significance of any appeal to history, including an apologetic one.

For what would the apologetic appeal to history be supposed to establish? Popper discusses the possibility of testability in the social sciences, which might include history, and at one point has the following passage, which seems to me to be very much relevant *ad rem*:

> The result of tests is the *selection* of hypotheses which have stood up to the tests, or the *elimination* of those hypotheses which have not stood up to them, and which are therefore rejected. It is important to realize the consequences of this view. They are these: all tests can be interpreted as attempts to weed out false theories – to find the weak points of a theory in order to reject it if it is falsified by the test. This view is sometimes considered paradoxical; our aim, it is said,

is to establish theories, not to eliminate false ones. But just because it is our aim to establish theories as well as we can, we must test them as severely as we can; that is, we must try to find fault with them, we must try to falsify them. Only if we cannot falsify them in spite of our best efforts can we say that they have stood up to severe tests. This is the reason why the discovery of instances which confirm a theory means very little if we have not tried, and failed, to discover refutations. For if we are uncritical we shall always find what we want: we shall look for, and find, confirmations, and we shall look away from, and not see, whatever might be dangerous to our pet theories. In this way it is only too easy to obtain what appears to be overwhelming evidence in favour of a theory which, if approached critically, would have been refuted.[3]

That, surely, strikes home with regard to so much Christian apologetic. This is the reason why the discovery of instances which confirm a theory means very little. For if we are uncritical we shall always find what we want. Whether or not we accept Popper's contention that theories can only be falsified and never verified – and I am extremely attracted to it (I think we can find out what God does not want; it is hellishly difficult to find out what he does want. We do that, of course, in heavenly hope, but that is by the way) – whether or not we accept Popper's contention that theories are in fact only kept going as long as they are not falsified and are fruitful in dealing with problems we want to deal with, Popper's description of the selective accumulation of supporting evidence clearly strikes home.

This, I would suggest, is a diagnostic feature of church history and indeed of the history of doctrine with regard to historical happenings and development. Instances of the sorts of things I have in mind are the following. First, the splendidly innocent affirmation at the beginning of the Preface of the Ordinal in the Book of Common Prayer, is typical of so many arguments about orders and the church: 'It is evident unto all men diligently reading Holy Scripture and ancient Authors that from the Apostles' time there have been these Orders of Ministers in Christ's Church; Bishops, Priests and Deacons.' This is the sort of thing which is referred to elsewhere as the threefold historical ministry and gets built into quadrilaterals and all sorts of other things. It is now almost universally admitted, certainly by Roman Catholic scholars and elsewhere, that no such thing is evident. Appeals to history, therefore, concerning the shape of the ministry of the church are all necessarily special pleading. It may or may not be appropriate, authentic and acceptable for there to be special pleading. But these cannot be straightforward descriptions or appeals to history without intervening interpretations and presuppositions. A case is being made and history, as well as being interpreted, is being made up with a view to influencing how history shall now go on.

I will repeat that. A case is being made and history, as well as being interpreted, is being made up with a view to influencing how history shall now go on. It seems to me that all books about and all argument about the ordering of the church (or of a church) are manifestly, and on simple inspection, of this nature.

Consider another area briefly, namely the commonplaces of Anglican church historians that both the evangelical and the tractarian movements were revivals which clearly contributed positively and in a godly manner to the survival and development of the Church of England through the nineteenth century and into the twentieth. This may be so, but it is not self-evident from a simple inspection of history and the present, especially when one sees how the Church of England through and in its General Synod is in danger of being paralysed about change because of the existence and sectarian activities of both the evangelical and the catholic parties. Of course, again, we have the other problem of continuity and identity, and it is not a simple matter to say that nineteenth-century evangelicals are found in the evangelical wing and mid-nineteenth-century tractarians are found in the Anglo-Catholic wing. But at least it can be alleged that this has contributed a cause to the present situation and there is some sort of continuing causal continuum. That, of course, is an interpretation of my own, but it does suggest another way of looking at nineteenth-century Anglican church history in England.

One could at least plausibly argue that the two trends as they developed into parties turned the Church of England more and more in on itself, made it more and more an institution concerned with inward-looking religion and deprived it of a central and communal capacity to change and adapt to the realistic demands of Christian mission in an increasingly secularized and industrial century. I will consider this further in my third lecture, but part of the evidence of this is that I continue to suspect that the vast majority of laymen do not care (if I may so put it) a damn for most of the things that the General Synod gets worked up about. Only those who get elected to it care – and they are thereby clericalized and corrupted by it.

I am making the point, simply, that church history is frequently more propaganda than realistically helpful and tends to assume that what happened must have happened for the best because it happened. This is a bit like arguments that the Russian revolution – including Stalin – demonstrate the truth of the revolutionary dialectic because it modernized backward Russia. But that fails to consider what other alternatives might have been possible, or whether the actual way things went was not much nearer to a disaster than a blessing. I am not, of course, suggesting that arguments about evangelicals and tractarians are like arguments about Stalin. I am simply throwing it into relief by raising the question whether it is not the case that what are called blessings might not actually be largely disasters.

All this, of course, is simply pointing to the problem of historical interpretation. Let me take a third and last case: the type of argument that is to be found in the Anglican/Roman Catholic International Commission's reports and the presuppositions that go round them and with them. We may take these as demonstrating that type of appeal to church history which assumes that of course what I may call the great churches are normative for models of the church and formative of our expectations of and organizing of the church today and looking towards the future. But how do we know this? Certainly not from a simple inspection of history. First, the so-called great churches are amazingly culture-shaped and culture-bound. Yet the culture and society which lie ahead of us, not to mention the culture and society which we have been living through for two hundred and fifty years are, as such, in acute discontinuity with the long culture of Christendom, and of Byzantium under Arabs and Turks, which shaped the great church. Why, therefore, should it be normative and formative for us? It is something to be argued.

Secondly, if the approval and providence of God is alleged to be claimed to give authority to all that the great churches have done, and all the attitudes that the great churches so frequently display, what are we to say about God?

Thirdly, how do we know that God was not and is not more decisively at work in what I might call the dispersed and diverse churches of non-conformity, dissent, pentecostalism and pluralism? If we do know, will it not be for theological reasons and for judgments about viability, authenticity for now and possibility for the future, rather than any simple reading of past history? And so on.

It is not at all evident that church history, as a series of selective raids on the past, is a decisive guide for decisions of faith in the present and organizing for worship in the future. Moreover, if there is such special pleading, might it not be symptomatic of an attempt to keep up appearances when, in fact, the whole credibility and plausibility of Christianity and the churches are being steadily undermined with the prospect of eventual disappearance or, at best, survival only as a religious hangover (like the very odd business of having the Bishop of Durham in the very odd business of the House of Lords)? The appeal to history, and more especially the way history is handled and presented, may not be apologetic at all. It may well be defensive and symptomatic of decay.

So in closing this lecture I think I must declare the basic

presuppositions with which I approach these issues. These are presuppositions of faith, arrived at and sustained by a contemporary piece of autobiographical history shared with, and shaped by, contemporary experiences of the community of faith (or one of the communities of faith) in today's world. These communities of faith are those which have the history and interpretation of their experiences of faith recorded in, and reflected by, the Bible. And these experiences came to be through and around my membership of, and participation in, that set of communities of faith which is organized more or less into and as that more or less recognizable historical entity and institution, the Church of England.

For me, all these experiences, their significance, their hope, their promise, are crucially and critically focussed, underlined and sustained by what I can best describe as the things to do with Jesus. I have found, and I continue to find, that the biblical stories and the things concerned with Jesus are profoundly resonant and therefore profoundly relevant to the way things go on in the world, the way things go wrong in the world and the way human beings can be offered hope and worth in and through the world and beyond the world. I believe, therefore, that the world, the universe and any personal beings anywhere in it (including those small earthly specks who are human beings) are open to a God of mystery, a God of grace, a God of presence and a God of action, the God to whom the biblical records and the accumulation of experience of tradition, spirituality, worship and practice of the Christian churches are distinctive, formative and necessary pointers. I believe myself to live, and I believe I can establish a reasonable claim to be living, within the ambit and the implications of the biblical witness to God. This being so, I am not able to rule out *a priori* any particular form or class of what I will rather deliberately call 'transactions', any class of transactions between this mysterious God and the derived mysteries who are human beings within the content of the world and the universe as we experience them, discover them and are shaped by them. I venture to state this rather baldly and without further argument or explanation so that it may be clear to any who care to give heed to these lectures on what basis I operate – that they are in fact a theological exploration in the interests of, and on the basis of, faith in God the Holy Trinity. They are not an enquiry as to whether such a faith is possible and legitimate. They are an exploration on the basis of such a faith.

This, together with my beginning, is I believe, highly relevant to the nature of apologetic, including the appeal to history as an integral part of Christian apologetic. It may have been supposed – I think, in some quarters (including those from which certain positions are urgently being argued at present) it is still supposed – that an appeal to history can establish overwhelmingly decisive arguments about what is now to be done in the church about order, about belief, about mission. It may further be held that by appealing to history, powerful apologetic arguments can be adduced which ought to convince reasonable men and women of good will of something like the proposition that Christianity is true. A theme which will be running through these lectures is the contention that this is a misunderstanding, a misunderstanding of how God, Christianity and history so to speak go together. (The second lecture will be discussing further how God, Christianity and history so to speak go together.) It is also a misunderstanding of how people come to faith, and of how faith develops and grows in the encounters of faithful and would-be faithful people with God in the world and with the goings-on which will presumably in due course themselves become – or can become – subjects or objects of history. What is clear (although many religious and Christian apologists reject or ignore this clarity and none of us have yet worked out its implications in any satisfactory way) is that all history is made up, and church history is made up more than most.

I mean primarily by this that all historical accounts are made-up compositions of selected fact and chosen interpretation. But I would like to keep operating in the background the suggestion that what you might call history itself – that is, the course of events, the interactions of human agents and sufferers with

56

what is going on – is made up as it goes along. That is to say, by their action and reaction to what is going on people as persons make a difference to what is going on.

One of the things that makes a difference in what is going on is the interpretations put on what is going on, the intentions they invest in such goings-on and the stories they tell themselves about what is going on. The 'making it up as you go along' is therefore an intrinsic element in history, both in the sense of historical accounts of what went on and in the sense of an at least informative element about what is actually going on.

The implications of this for an appeal to history as an integral part of Christian apologetic is that such an appeal cannot lay claim to an absolutely acceptable weight or to any validity which is generally, publicly compelling. It depends on how you look at things – on the pressures to and from which you choose; on the stories by which you select facts. It depends, too, on the philosophy, ideology, myth or story by which you are claimed and to which you give your commitment. For future reference I should just register the point that this does not mean that everyone is free to make up any story he or she likes, and all known knowledge and claim is purely subjective and wholly relative. Goings-on are there in the sense that they are given independently to the observers, even if the observers are not able to pick them up without some interpretation. People are there, and I continue obstinately to believe that God is there (we will waive that one, though – it is good enough to agree on the things and people!). There is a being-up-againstness of things, events and persons which can be gainsaid only at great and destructive cost. So it does not mean that all objectivity has gone out of the window, but it does mean that objectivity is not as objective as many people think, many theorists postulate and many arguments assume.

So, apologetic arguments, and in particular arguments which appeal to history, are not and cannot be cast-iron defence of things alleged to be derived from history or established by history. Nor can they provide compelling proofs of what should now be taken as truth, or held to be the proper and necessary ways of doing this or expressing that – or turning this insight of men and women into the universe into a way of life; or, indeed, deciding about the life and ordering of the church or a church. Appeals to history can only be current and contemporary explanations and expositions of what is understood, believed and claimed as received from the past for use, interpretation and further experimentation now with a view to the future. Such apologetic can be only exploratory, explanatory and persuasive. If other people can be brought to see certain things in a certain light, then maybe they will come to share in that way of receiving things and to commit themselves to the communal practices and exploration of that way of looking at things. (I am here describing one of the ways into Christian faith through, for example, an 'apologetic appeal to history'.)

Apologetic, then, is not and cannot be to do with proof and decisive demonstration, but only to do with persuasion and explanatory exploration. This becomes clear when we face up to the selective and propagandist nature of all church history. But this is not a destructive conclusion nor scarcely, even, a disturbing conclusion. For surely persuasion and patiently collaborative exploration are just the sort of approaches Christian believers ought to find appropriate to a God who has risked himself in creation and risked identifying himself in history in a serving and suffering human being.

# 2

## *Historicism and Acts of God*

This lecture is largely a thought-experiment conducted around
the question 'Did God push the Emperor Theodosius off his
horse on 28 July 450?' The purpose of the thought-experiment
is to see whether we can gather some articulated suggestions
which have some coherence and some persuasiveness about
any sense in which God can be said to be active in history or, as
I suggested very briefly in my last lecture, God can be said to
be transactive – or perhaps interactive – with human beings in
history. We should then be describing, or at least sketching
out, a possible model, or set of models, for making claims
about ways in which God, human beings and causes and events
in history go together, i.e. coalesce, so that it may properly and
practically be claimed that a purpose can be at work in history
– or that in and through history purposes may be detected,
either as individuals or as formed into various groupings. If we
could do that, we would then be sketching out some linkages
by which talking about Providence in history could be related
to talking about accidents in history. The purpose and focus of
this exercise in the general theological area of providence is to
give those of us to whom it is a matter of concern some
coherent and explicated way of addressing practical questions
about the identity of the Church of England, the nature of
Anglicanism and the bearing of this on questions about which
decisions have to be taken within the Church of England and
within the Anglican Communion in the near future. It might

also enable us to pick up and tidy up the rather unsatisfactory state in which I left church history at the end of my first lecture.

Of course, any success that this or a similar enterprise could have would depend on its being plausible and credible to hang on to the conviction that there is a God of whom it can be appropriately, authentically and practically said that he (or she or it? or all three?) transacts or interacts with the world in a manner which is analogous to the personal and in a manner which can be detected and responded to by persons. Obviously, very, very many people do not hold this belief, including some who hold themselves to be firmly and rightly within the biblical and Christian traditions of belief in, exploration into and response to God. With such people I am not at present directly arguing. It may be that these lectures will illuminate that clash of belief obiquely by pointing to possible ways of going on talking about a 'personal' God which lessen the difficulties that some people see with such a belief and such language. If this were so, it would be an example of that persuasive but non-decisive apologetic of which I spoke at the end of my first lecture.

So having, I hope, sufficiently set the context of my thought-experiment, let us pursue it. As an 'ideal-type' specimen question about the relationship of the God of the biblical and Christian traditions to history consider: 'Did God push the Emperor Theodosius off his horse on 28 July 450?' You will, I am sure, have already sensed that my answer to that question is an unambiguous 'No'. According to such evidence as we have and any reasonable assessment of the event the Emperor fell off his horse by accident. If we ask why the accident happened, the answer (supposing there was enough evidence available to give us an answer) would probably be something like: 'the horse stumbled or shied and the Emperor, by reason of increasing age and infirmity, was unable to keep his seat and fell off in such a manner that, being a heavy man (?), he killed himself.' Such an account would be typical of accidents involving human beings. A random event (triggered off by a series of other random events – why did the horse shy, etc., etc.?) causes

60

another event which triggers off an example of some pretty general and, from the historical point of view, pretty trivial general laws. (Old age weakens people's power, including the power to hold one's seat on a shying horse; heaviness increases effects of impacts from a height, etc.)

Of course, the concept of 'a random event' is philosophically a rather tricky one, but for our purposes we can stick with the judgment that the event was an 'accident' because we have no grounds for entertaining the hypothesis that the set of causes which led up to the event had in them a willed act or acts which intended the end that either Theodosius should fall off his horse or that that should kill him. So it was an accident.

It is worth noting that even if Theodosius's fall from his horse had been the result of an assassination attempt, it would still be an accident from the point of view of the set of events which interest us – namely, those events which resulted in the adoption of the Chalcedonian Definition of the Person of Christ. At least, it would still be an accident unless there were grounds for supposing that the hypothetical assassination attempt were engineered in some way by a person or persons intending to promote the cause of Leo and the christology of the *Tomus ad Flavianum.* Such evidence, if it existed, would not, I fancy, plausibly help the cause either of God or of providence. However, a speculation of this sort may help us to see that the question of whether a certain event or cluster of events is to be received and responded to as purposive or as accidental depends upon what sort of reasonably coherent sub-system of interlocking events and causes an observer or participant is able reasonably to construct. Moveover, an event can fit into two or more sub-systems and 'look differently' with regard to purpose and accident in the different sub-systems.

In our hypothetical example let us suppose, for the sake of our thought experiment, that the Emperor Theodosius's fatal fall from his horse was engineered by a party of conspirators who intended to overthrow him but who were not in the least concerned about ecclesiastical controversies over obscure points to do with the nature and being of Christ. Then, within the sub-system that was focussed on the court and political history of the fifth-century Roman empire, the Emperor's death would be purposive and not an accident. It was the result of intentionality, directed to that very end for wider purposes and aims. Even so, within the sub-system of events and causes which was focussed on the history of Christian doctrine, or on church history aligned on the problem of the power, influence and office of the Popes of Rome, the emperor's death would still be an accident. Nobody whose intentionality was committed to doctrinal controversies or to the power of the Roman See had anything to do with its causes; only with the opportunities provided by its effects. As far as they were concerned, therefore, it was an accident – even if it turned out to be a very fortunate accident.

Leaving aside this entirely imaginary hypothesis about assassination, which was introduced purely to illustrate the notion of events being accidential in some sub-systems and the same events being purposive in others, let us concentrate on the question of an accident which is received as a fortunate accident. Were the proponents of the See of Rome – or those who came to regard the Chalcedonian Definition as the very pillar and bastion of orthodoxy – entitled to thank God for this accident, and if so, what would they be thanking God for? Clearly not for pushing the Emperor Theodosius off his horse or for putting people up to activities which caused him to fall off his horse.

All this may seem to be painfully obvious to many people, but I am afraid that many discussions, some of which are of considerable practical importance, are conducted about church history, about Christian doctrine and about the current ordering of the church or a church on unclarified or unnamed assumptions about God's relation to the causes and events which are the subject-matter of history which are as crude as the instance I am discussing. It may be easier to seek to clarify this issue around what for most people is a fairly remote example than to seek to do so about the alleged form of acts of God in history which are widely held to be much nearer the heart of the symbolism of the Christian faith and story about God, men and women and the world.

I suggest, therefore, that it is necessary to be quite clear that there are at least three reasons of three very different types for rejecting the notion that God's actions, transactions or interactions with human beings and with the goings-on of history can be conceived of, in any simple or simply identifiable sense as directly causal. God did not push the Emperor Theodosius off his horse nor bring it about that other sets of events caused the Emperor Theodosius to fall off his horse and be killed. The reasons why believers in a God who transacts and interacts with women and men in and through history must unambiguously reject this notion in any form are as follows.

The first reason is a moral reason and may be indicated thus. A God who uses the openness of his created universe, the openness and freedom of men and women created in his image and the mystery of his own risky and creative love to insert additional causal events from time to time into that universe to produce particular events or trends by that eventuality alone would be a meddling demigod, a moral monster and a contradiction of himself. I know that this assertion causes great disturbance and distress among many Christian believers, including not a few whom I personally greatly respect as believers and disciples. But it has to be made. Unless we can be clear that between the scientific and historical causalities of the universe and of the world on the one hand and the actions and transactions of God with persons on the other there is a space, then the problem of evil is absolutely overwhelming. I personally would sympathize with those who find evil overwhelming in any case. But as a Christian who believes that there is a real and basic sense in which God interacts with the world as he is in Jesus, I do not believe this. Nonetheless I am increasingly clear that God is not an arbitrary meddler nor an occasional fixer. This is morally intolerable, and no appeal to the mysteriousness of particularity or its scandal can overcome this. God is no more and no less directly concerned with the death of the Emperor Theodosius as an event in history than he is with the death of anyone else. However he interacts or transacts he cannot intervene as an additional inserted and occasional historical cause.

Which leads into the second type of reason for rejecting this notion, which is a theological one. This is very far-reaching, but can be stated only baldy and briefly. Let it be supposed, as I suppose and believe, that the stories in and of the Bible – in the first place, in and of the Old Testament – reflect a set of experiences of, and interactions with, the God of the universe. These stories are rightly responded to as normative for, and formative of, continuing sets of responses to and transactions with that God in the ongoing stuff of history. Let it further be supposed – and this I take to be a supposition which must be shared by every Christian as a basic matter of definition – that the experiences and the story of Jesus are decisive for a definitive turn in the story about, and the experiences of, the normative and formative comings together of this God and men and women in the world and in history. Then it surely becomes clear that the God who is held to be in some decisive sense the author of the whole story, in some real sense the basic presence in and animateur of the whole story, and in some truly imposing sense the purpose and possibility of the entire story, when and if it reaches its end – that this God cannot and ought not to be thought of and where necessary argued about as if he were the supreme *controller* of the universe who *manages* its affairs by a series of direct interventions for which he alone is responsible and to which response is inevitable in a cause-and-effect way. He is a God of open personal transactions who insists and persists in a self-giving way of risk, and self-denying way of invitation that has not yet established anything like a total persuasive sway over or in a universe which – to borrow Austin Farrer's phrase – God has made so that it has to make itself.

Thus the implications of any story about God, men and women and the world which is evoked, shaped and sustained by a readiness to explore the impact and cohesiveness of biblical experiences, focussed and redirected by the Jesus story, are

64

that God is like a mysterious artist who moves towards the achievement of the dreams and the purposes of his artistry by committing himself to his material as a suffering servant. He is much more like this than he is like an emperor of celestial dimensions and of universal and meticulous bureaucratic manipulation.

If I had the time, I would pursue this line of thought by arguing that one could reasonably conclude that the increasing stripping from all the Christian churches of the culturally acquired pretensions to power in, and dominance over, the way men and women look at the world and the ways in which societies are supposed to run is precisely a 'providential' development – the effects of a set of historical accidents and trends which free believers in the God of the story of Jesus from delusions of grandeur and offer them a compelling opportunity to come to terms with the possibilities of interaction and transaction with this servant God, a servant God who has been far too shut up in, and equated with, culturally determined models of empire, power and control. However, I do not have time to develop this, so I move to my third type of argument.

This is a logical argument which is, I think, independent of moral and theological considerations in any direct way. It has to do with the impropriety of any argument which seeks to establish from the observation of unique or singular historical events a claim about the way things are going – or are being made to go – in history. That is to say that if there *is* a claim to discern what is 'really going on' in history, or to be able to discern, say, the revelatory import of an event or set of events in history, then it is not a historical claim; it cannot be validated by further raids into history and it certainly cannot refer to a general direction of history.

This is the whole matter of historicism, which as I said in the last lecture, took Sir Karl Popper a complete book to explain and expose. However, for the purposes of these lectures, I think I can sufficiently indicate the directions in which I would work out the argument by two observations. The first picks up the point I made earlier about an event being purposive in one sub-system of interest and explanation and accidental in other such sub-systems. This, I think, points to the conclusion that the detection and implication of a purposive direction in events depends on a perspective of interest and on a capacity to select a small enough sub-system or network of events and causes within it, which makes sense to talk about purposes or intentions of human agents – themselves acting as causes of events or as effecting causal chains of events. The capacity to talk effectively about purposive direction is lost once one goes beyond any particular selected sub-system, and certainly cannot be sustained if one starts to imagine that there is a purposive and directional system which contains and controls all sub-systems. Such an approach can only be a pure effort of imagination, and it cannot have any practical or logically sustainable applications. On the one hand there is no perspective available which provides the conspectus required or includes a capacity to spot the intentional action of a coherent and cohering agent who is exercising what we can recognize as intentionality throughout, and in relation to, all the causal chains of events. On the other hand, we have already observed that actual events are accidental from one point of view and purposive from another. It is therefore incoherent to suppose that there is a 'higher point of view' which makes them all purposive – for purpose can be detected only at the level where there are different points of view. I suspect that this in some way ties up with my first point about the immorality of consecrating arbitrariness, but I cannot pursue this. We must, I think, be clear that history is not a system but an immensely varied series of causes and events which can be selected and sorted out in an immense variety of ways according to authentic and disciplined selections of particular interests in 'what happened then' and in 'what we are concerned about now'. It is not, therefore, possible to read the whole of history in terms of the activities of a purposive God or in terms of any other all-embracing and allegedly overriding theory, faith or ideology.

If therefore we do, for reasons of faith and belief, continue to hold that there is some sense in which interaction with God is a direct and effective possiblity within the goings-on of our lives which are part of history and that things have been experienced and learnt in the past which help us about these interactions and transactions of God, we have to be clear that this is not because God has inserted additional causes into the ordinary cause-and-effect chains of history. The failure of historicism to be logical or sustainable or desirable rules out any simplistic notion of acts of God as direct and historical. (It does not rule out a powerful symbolic role for such a notion, but we cannot pursue that now.)

The way forward lies along the lines of narrative, story, tradition and contemporary practice, together with the notion of space – which I introduced above in my outlining of the moral argument against attribution of direct causal acts to God. I have time only for a brief sketch of an approach which I shall seek to develop and consolidate in the last two lectures as I work it out in direct relationship to the emergence and future of the Church of England and of Anglicanism.

My suggestion is that 'history' is what we, as human beings, are just about able to make it – except as and when history not so much overtakes us as overcomes us. That is to say that our human lives within the goings-on both of the phenomena properly studied by science and of the historical happenings which are delved into by historians and social scientists are open to possibilities of purpose, direction and promise. This is so, however, not because of anything that is either divinely or materially programmed into the goings-on. It is because men and women (and any other personal-type beings who might possibly exist anywhere else) have emerged with the capacity so to stand in the goings-on that they also stand out of them. (Possibilities of self-consciousness, freedom and becoming initiatory causes as well as reactive events and processes are indicators of this.) This 'standing out' of persons enables (although it does not compel) interactions or transactions with God who may be conceived as a power behind all that is, a presence within all that is and a promise beyond all that is, who as such 'stands out' (that is, in traditional language, is

67

transcendent) with a capacity to stand in. The interactions and transactions, however, have to be conceived of as occurring in a maintained and privileged space which, so to speak, holds apart or allows autonomy to the goings-on of science and history, the personal lives of human beings and the independent existence of God. This notion of space is a way of pointing to the inevitable mystery of the transactions and interactions between God, personal beings and the goings-on of the world and history. This mystery means that neither the core nor the construction of the mystery is available to us. (We can never pin down what God – or what a human being – really and exhaustively is, any more than we can exhaustively or definitively describe how the goings-on actually and finally come together or precisely how 'it', whatever 'it' is, works.) This could be worked out with regard to miracles – which I believe happen – although one can never tell until afterwards that they have happened, only some people recognize them as miracles, and you can never tell how they happen – though you can have some idea of how they did not happen. (For example, they do not happen by physical manipulation, see the whole discussion above.) What we do know about (some of us) is part of the reality, and some of the effects, of the mysterious but real transactions and interactions.

It would not, however, be possible to put up this descriptive quasi-theory or be engaged in the task of seeing how it works out if one had not been caught up by and caught up into the story about God, men and women and the world which is some version or other of the interweaving effect of the biblical stories and, within them and in reaction to them, the stories about Jesus. This is the tradition of stories which is definitive for – but by no means, alas, systematically formative of the Christian churches. The challenges and opportunities of the Christian churches and of Christians are to take part in the shaping of the stories of human living in the world by taking part in shaping and being shaped by the stories which arise out of the biblical stories in relation to the living of the church in the goings-on of the world – all as part of renewed and renewing transactions and interactions with God.

As a preparation for my trying to make this clearer and more concrete in my last two lectures, note finally the following. First, *providence* might be conceived of as the possible inter-action of the mystery of God with the mystery of human beings in the midst of what goes on in that created space which is occupied by the material of science and of history. It could point to the continuing possibility repeatedly but very partially actualized in limited particulars where persons make sense of what happens in terms of a story which both gives meaning to, and makes meaning of, human living in the context of God who has been involved in transactions which give us clues to the story within the story.

Secondly, to approach human living, history, accident and providence along the lines of an emerging divine and human narrative or story allows the combination of unpredictability with an ongoing purpose. This avoids any suggestion of his-toricism. What happens in history is what happens in history, and it is quite as likely to be the unexpected as the expected. Stories can make themselves up as they go along, and this can go along with actors and authors contributing to the story for continuing and ever-steadfast purposes, which will nonetheless have to be continuously adapted, and adaptable for, what happens. 'Providence' need not mean either tight control or intervening arbitrariness.

Thirdly, and finally, and with practical reference to the appli-cation of so-called historical arguments to current ecclesiastical controversies about the ordering and defining either of belief or of the church, it is very important to note the following. It may be – for the immediately foreseeable future it certainly will be – that very many people who are powerful Christian believers and very active in church affairs will vehemently maintain that my rejection of acts of God as direct causal interventions in the events of history is faithless and under-mining of the very nature of Christian faith. This will be an exploration into faith and its implications which will have to go on. (Consider again the next two lectures.) But within a story there is nothing contradictory to the logic and direction of the story in having to argue within it what it is really about and how it is going to develop. This argument, that is, about what can be meant by acts of God, will certainly go on, and my version, even if more fully and carefully worked out, will certainly not prove anything like universally acceptable. But the point with regard to ecclesiastical controversies and appeals to history, including apologetic ones, is this.

Whatever may be claimed about a certain special, limited class of events, held to be acts of God, the arguments which I have outlined at least show that the logical and causal links between any such special class and what we now have to decide about belief in the church and the ordering of the church are too precarious and too incapable of being stated clearly, decisively and with universal agreement to permit the reference to them as direct sources for deduction about how we now go on. Arguments about the current ordering of the church, however they are related to the past, cannot be determined by alleged narrative events in the past and alleged causative links between these events and now which predictably bind us and must bind us for the future. Claiming this sort of thing is logically and historically unsustainable and theologically and practically undesirable and dangerous.

At one point in a brilliant discussion of tradition in his book *After Virtue*, to which I shall have occasion to return, Alasdair MacIntyre remarks: 'When men and women identify what are in fact their partial and particular causes too easily and too completely with the cause of some universal principle, they usually behave worse than they would otherwise do.'[1]

That, I am afraid, is one of the things that church history *does* teach us – and it is one of the things which is in grave danger of being illustrated in the current controversies in the General Synod of the Church of England and the Church of England at large.

# 3

## *The Emergence of Anglicanism*

Let me remind you that what I am attempting to do is to carry out a Christian theological investigation. My basis is one of sharing in the faith of that community of communities who believe in the reality and activity of God, the reality and the activity of the God who is pointed to, and reflected in and by, the stories and patterns and prayers of the Bible. These stories and patterns and prayers are believed to have been decisively focussed, and given their direction, by Jesus and the things to do with him. Of course one has to be clear that these things to do with Jesus are likewise known to us by stories and patterns and prayers.

I think that one of the things that I am arguing and trying to take into account is that you cannot get outside the stories and patterns and prayers to things and events on which they are based and which are perceived and known independently of the stories and patterns and prayers. That is to say that there is a peculiar and important sense in which the objective and the subjective cannot be separated. (In fact it has occurred to me, as I have been writing these lectures, that I am in fact sketching out an epistemology – but I won't pursue epistemology to-night; I shall just assume that I know what I don't know, but what I live by.)

I start from the conviction, which I hold to be persuasively related to (although not proved by) actual experience, that the God of the biblical patterns and the things concerning Jesus reflect and point to actual and continuing possibilities in the goings on which make up the world and the universe as we experience them. That is to say, that a biblical and Christian faith holds that the things concerning God and Jesus are in some real way connected to and interactive with the things pursued in the study of science and those events pursued in the study of history: those things, in other words, which constitute the continuum of the world as we live in it.

The point is, how are they connected and how do they interact? I have taken as an instance of these questions: How are the accidents of history related to the providence of God? Hence my sketches in the first two lectures: first the nature and operations of church history and secondly the question of acts of God and historicism. People tell selective stories from, or of, church history, at least for reasons of controversy and not infrequently for purposes of propaganda. In so far as these are claimed to be about what God is to be discerned to have done, they are also claimed to be relevant to decisions about what God would have us do now. This is the point. The whole set of arguments and argumentations, controversy, propaganda, although they are alleged to be to do with the past, are of course to do with what we should do now – or more often, being the church, what we should not do now. As an old friend of mine got up and told the General Synod once: there is nothing in the New Testament against doing a thing for the first time. Many people believe there is, of course.

As this is what the arguments are used for, it is necessary to consider controversial appeals to church history in the light of considerations about what we can now reasonably mean or intend by discerning God as active in, or active in relation to, particular historical events or allegedly discernible historical trends or tendencies. That was what I was discussing in my first lecture. In my second lecture I sketched out an argument for maintaining that we cannot and must not claim that God as it were adds events to history, or directly intervenes to produce trends and tendencies in history by behaving as an additional or special cause in a cause-and-event chain. I suggested, rather, than those of us who do believe that God interacts with and transacts within history will have to operate with some notion of a mystery of structured space, a structured space which is to be encountered and experienced by persons within the stuff of science and within the events of history. This structured space is where interaction and transactions between persons and God can personally and really occur. The mystery and the space is where we who stand in history and matter can stand out and encounter the transcendent mystery of God, God who none-theless transcends his transcendence so that he can stand in.

This is my attempt to relate the implications and experiences of the stories, patterns and prayers of the Bible to what we must now reasonably understand about the goings-on of both science and history. In particular, it is my attempt to respond to what I regard as the totally unsatisfactory nature of any forms of direct interventionism or historicism.

At the end of my last lecture I finally pointed out that it would no doubt continue to be urged by many Christian controversialists and decision-takers that a biblical faith ob-liged one to preserve a certain class of quasi-unique events, perhaps very limited, which were interventions of God in history in a straightforward way. I argued that even so, such a class of events could not be used for historical arguments or as analogues, or anologies, or models, to give any decisive line on interpreting or responding to historical events in general – including church historical events. In other words, I wanted to contend as a so-to-speak weaker version of my case – let us suppose that the case about direct interventions on certain unique occasions remains open; they are such a set of unique occasions that they do not allow us then to go on arguing about historical trends and events. They only give us clues, if you allow this case, to the way in which we should respond to historical events and so on.

I would sum up what I am after in the arguments and explorations of these lectures by saying that it may be possible to read providence into events so far in relation to taking decisions now, with a view to maintaining purpose and direction in the future. This might be done by reference to a set of stories and patterns and prayers, of which one believed oneself to be a part, and which amounted to a narrative about the way things were meant to go, ought to go, and might be made to go. In the light of these patterns and of the directionality of the narrative we could choose, out of what has been accidentally developed in the past, what is useful to us for now and the future. Useful would mean useful for developing the narrative further in the combined story-making between God and women and men. Purpose, as I suggested at the end of the last lecture, could be pursued without assuming any guaranteed particular predictability and therefore claiming, for instance, that if we do this we are bound to be doing God's will, or alternatively, flouting God's will. We don't know; we can only try and find out.

It is not, however, legitimate, prudent or desirable to read any determining providence *out of* events of history so far. The effect of that would be to declare that the past (or what is always called the past, but is more properly selective events from, or views on, the past) is held to be in some way binding on the present. Nor must we hold that the pious past is either decisive for, or guaranteeing of, any particular shape of the future. History continues to be accidental. If it is open to purpose, it is so only in and through the interaction of the personal mystery of human beings with the mystery of God in, and in relation to, the goings-on of history. Faith, it seems clear to me, cannot eliminate risk or blunt the autonomies of creative realities.

Which brings me to the particular object of my enquiries into historical accident and personal providence. What is to be made of the emergence, and of the future, of the Church of England and of Anglicanism?

I suggest that some such approach as I am outlining sets those of us who care about the Church of England free to be both realistic and yet responsible and hopeful about it within the purposes and providence of God. I agree, of course, that this takes some believing, but I continue to try. It is obvious, in fact, that I am both prejudiced here and must declare an interest. I have received my encounters with God, my calling to respond to God and the shaping of my understanding of what it is to worship God and to have hope in God largely and basically through and in the Church of England. I chose to become a member of the Church of England (I was raised a Methodist and I could discuss the accidents by which I became a member of the Church of England some time if it were thought to be relevant); I believed I was called to be a priest in the church of God through the Church of England and when, by a combination of divine providence and prime ministerial inadvertence, I was asked to be a bishop in the Church of England it seemed to me (and I am bound to say, it seemed also to my wife – or I wouldn't have done it) to be my plain and simple duty to accept this calling also. Therefore I am bound to do all I can to fit the Church of England into God's providence. Let us be clear about that.

It is for readers to decide whether my special pleading is too special and beyond the reasonable bounds of reason, of theology and of common sense. As I understand it, I am trying to make sense of what has happened to me in the light of insights from the Christian story and patterns and prayer, as I have received them largely, but by no means exclusively, through the Church of England, and in response to experience and practice as I have been caught up in them, and with the help of all the resources of observation, analysis and rationality that are available to me. In this I believe and hope that I am firmly in a central Church of England tradition of appealing to, and working with, the biblical witness, the traditions of the Fathers and of the church, and the sound use of reason. But I may, of course, be overwhelmingly involved in special pleading, special pleading to maintain my own collusive fantasy with those who wish to maintain the Church of England as a cosy club against the erosions of modernity and the threats of the future.

There is no way of becoming reasonably clear about this without the exposure of one's presuppositions, argumentation and conclusions to a wider public and to secular as well as to religious criticism. Will the arguments stand up at all to exposure? Do they have any sort of persuasive force? Even if they are not acceptable or must be left in suspense, do they resonate at all with the experiences and judgments from other perspectives of human experience – let alone from other perspectives of religious or Christian experience?

These sorts of questions show the relevance of the enquiry into apologetic as it is required of a Hensley Henson lecturer. It is necessary to give reasons for the faith that is in one. This is a necessity as much so that there may be a realistic development of that faith as so that one may put forward a persuasive presentation of it. If God is, and is indeed God, then those who would tentatively and fearfully argue or explore about him from their partial, particular and even accidental viewpoints must look for some signs, tests, suggestions that they are on to a wavelength and a resonance which goes far wider than their particular partialities or limited (and often limiting) experience.

So the attempt to be apologetic and explanatory and persuasive is an essential attempt of any sort of realistic faith. All this by way of preparing to face the surely and simply obvious fact that if anything is an accident of history the Church of England is. Consequently, this is all the more true of what has quite recently emerged and been called the Anglican Communion. The various Acts of Parliament and Royal determinations which shaped and reshaped the Church of England, gave it its liturgy and Prayer Book, and settled its Articles of Faith, are all clearly highly political in themselves and also much influenced by the changes and chances of political events which came between the various stages. These various stages move from Henry VIII's first interventions through the Elizabethan Settlement to the Prayer Book and Act of Uniformity under Charles II in 1662. Of course religion and politics were inextricably mixed. On the one hand what had come to be regarded as the godly prince was the determining authority throughout and no one doubted that church and state were two sides of one coin. On the other hand deep religious changes, explorations and renewals were at work, and men of searching authority and devout faith were involved in the work of developing the Church of England, a task which was set them by the godly prince. No one could accuse Cranmer or Parker or Laud of being unconcernd with faith, devotion and theology. They all struggled to do what they did in the firm belief that they were seeking to serve God and his church. But the outcomes of their various struggles, and the interaction between crown and bishops and Parliament, were clearly a series of political outcomes.

At the beginning of his first chapter on the Reformation in England in *The Reformation*, his volume in the Pelican History of the Church, Professor Owen Chadwick writes: 'England was unique in its Reformation, unique in the Church established in consequence of the Reformation.' In case this should raise ungodly pride, he then goes on: 'The English Reformation was emphatically a political revolution, and its author King Henry VIII resisted, for a time ferociously, many of the religious consequences which accompanied the legal changes everywhere else in Europe.'[1] Later, he draws attention to the reasons of state for the Elizabethan Settlement like this: 'Like Catherine de' Medici under the threat of civil war in 1562, like William the Silent when the Netherlands were being torn apart, like the Swedish kings' [quite a list of godly princes!], 'the English government sought for a moderate constitution, sufficiently reformed to satisfy reasonable Protestants, sufficiently conservative to satisfy the Catholics who were not determined to be Papists ... From motives of policy and personal inclination, and with the opinions of the country divided by the religious see-saw from Henry VIII to Mary, Queen Elizabeth of England intended to hold together, in an eternal conformity of moderation' [what a motto for the House of Bishops!] 'persons whose opinions might differ as widely as Lutheran differed from Calvinist.'[2] Although historical events had changed contexts and possibilities a good deal by the time we come to 1662, the same reasons of state for religious settlements had echoes in His Majesty's Declaration, prefaced to the republication with the Revised Prayer Book, under the Act of Uniformity, of the Thirty-Nine Articles of Religion.

Let me quote you two interesting paragraphs from that on the whole fairly rarely read document.

Being by God's Ordinance, according to Our just Title, Defender of the Faith, and Supreme Governor of the Church, within these Our Dominions, We hold it most agreeable to this Our Kingly Office, and Our own religious Zeal, to conserve and maintain the Church committed to Our Charge, in Unity of true Religion, and in the Bond of Peace; and not to suffer unnecessary Disputations, Altercations, or Questions to be raised, which may nourish Faction both in the Church and Commonwealth. We have therefore, upon mature Deliberation, and with the Advice of so many of Our Bishops as might conveniently be called together – [what if they missed the train to London, you see?] – thought fit to make this Declaration following:

Then there is the declaration, and in the middle of it this interesting paragraph:

That for the present, though some differences have been ill raised, yet We take comfort in this, that all Clergymen within Our Realm have always most willingly subscribed to the Articles established; which is an argument to Us, that they all agree in the true, usual, literal meaning of the said Articles; and that even in those curious points, in which the present differences lie, men of all sorts take the Articles of the Church of England to be for them which is an argument again, that none of them intend any desertion of the Articles established,

That therefore in these both curious and unhappy differences, which have for so many hundred years, in different times and places, exercised the Church of Christ, We will, that all further curious search be laid aside, and these disputes shut up in God's promises, as they be generally set forth to us in the Holy Scriptures, and the general meaning of the Articles of the Church of England according to them.

No wonder that bishops, generally speaking, are generally speaking! The object of the religious declarations and definitions of the Church of England is that there should be the one church in the one realm under the one crown and that all should belong to it. It is not to further either Lutheran or Calvinist doctrine, nor primarily to further Catholic order, but to maintain the religious and ecclesiastical unity of a Christian realm.

But history was already playing tricks with this and was about to play further tricks. By 1662 several things had left lasting impressions. The papal excommunication of Elizabeth and the Marian burnings – both of men and women and of the Prayer Book – had ensured that all Roman Catholics were potential, if not actual, traitors to the realm and objects of great public suspicion, even hatred. The Prayer Book was a principal symbol of what the Church of England stood for and was regarded as. It was, however, more a historic symbol than a theological or liturgical one, however much it did have, mercifully, its own theological and liturgical tone. This symbolic importance was reinforced by the outlawing of the Prayer Book and the persecution of its users under the Directory and under Cromwell. At the same time, those who were inclined to a Reformed theology, people whom the Elizabethan Settlement had attempted to keep within the church, these people were now tarred with the brush of the revolution and of the independents. So the restored Church of England was maintained by the godly prince (in the implausible form of Charles II) and Parliament together as the one church of a Christian realm. That was established by the Act of Uniformity and the Book of Common Prayer. But this church was increasingly failing to meet this prescription in practice. Roman Catholics were out on the one hand and the Reformed, together with the Independents and the Baptists and the Quakers, were out on the other. Before long, of course, many more people would be out for secular reasons, but this still lay in the future.

The Stuarts' hankering after Rome led to the so-called Glorious Revolution of 1688, and it is already clear, as we approach 1988, that people are discussing how glorious it was. But the Glorious Revolution led to the invitation from Parliament to William and Mary to take on the crown of England. The godly prince had deserted the church which had been established in and for the state by the line from Henry VIII through Elizabeth I and James I and Charles II, and the Non-Jurors felt obliged to take their undoubted piety, devotion and learning out of the life of the church because they could not forswear their oaths of allegiance to a legitimate sovereign. The new sovereign took a new coronation oath, to maintain the Protestant reformed religion established by law, and the law was maintained by Parliament. Is the identity of the Church of England, then, a parliamentary identity, and has Parliament inherited the role of the godly prince? Mr Enoch Powell, I think, and perhaps Mr John Selwyn Gummer may think so. In any case, this question is certainly still around after a first attempt to challenge it had been made by the Tractarians in the 1830s and 1840s. I will return to this.

First, however, three more points to notice in this necessarily eclectic survey of the complicated web of historical accidents which caused and shaped the Church of England. In 1662 the Church of England was fully re-established as the church of the realm of England with the famous Book of Common Prayer duly revised, issued and endorsed. Yet by 1689 it was made legally clear that whatever might be the established position of the Church of England in law, the prescription did not correspond to the descriptive position. As I have already pointed out, it never really had done. The differences between the prescription and the description had steadily widened as the events of history increased both the numbers and the variety of the recusants and the dissenters.

Now, on the verge of the century of the Enlightenment and of increasing secularization, the new government of William III and the Parliament which had invited him passed the Third Toleration Act, in 1689. It did not go very far, and attempts also to produce a Comprehension Bill which would ease non-conformists back into the Church of England by allowing a measure of laxity (a measure of laxity in relation to those symbolic stumbling-blocks of the sign of the cross in baptism, kneeling to receive holy communion and the wearing of the surplice) got lost in the rumblings of the revived convocation of the clergy. Here change was prevented because while some argued these things were in themselves indifferent, others talked threateningly about the thin end of the wedge and the dangers to the true nature of the church. High church clergy were deeply suspicious of latitudinarian bishops (a pattern which has been repeated on and off, come to think about it). Further, in practice dissenters were harassed and excluded from public office at all levels and things got worse again under Queen Anne, although they never returned to the severities of the Clarendon Code under Charles II. Nonetheless it was now clear from the statute book that church and realm were not one. It was not yet clear that being a citizen was not the equivalent of being a Christian. Indeed, professed non-Christians were not admitted to Parliament until late into the nineteenth century. But the erosion of one, never fully actualized, theoretical basis of the Church of England was now officially recognized. We clearly still have unfinished business here. In practice, both the Chuch of England and the state, despite their dependence on history and their appeals to history and tradition, are very slow to recognize what history has actually produced.

The further point is that the Toleration Act did not go with a spread of the spirit of tolerance. High churchmen under Queen Ann did their best to close up even dubious loopholes by which dissenters could occasionally conform and so partake to some extent in public life. Bitterness against the Church of England and fervent activities on behalf of the privileges of the Church of England on the part of bishops, parochial clergy and some laity continued to be a feature of religious life until we get the bitter anti-church feelings and campaigns of the nineteenth century. It should be noted, however, that this determination not to tolerate rivals was not confined to the Church of England. In Scotland there was much persecution of the continuing episcopalians, heightened no doubt by their being taken as loyal to the Catholic Stuarts. In 1703 a Bill for the Toleration of Dissenters was introduced in the Scottish Parliament where, of course, the Presbyterians were established and the rest dissenters. A petition against this bill stated that the petitioners produced the petition, as follows: 'Being persuaded that in the present case and circumstances of this church and nation' [this being, of course a Presbyterian church and nation] 'to enact a Toleration for those of that way *would be to establish iniquity by law* and would bring upon the promoters thereof and upon their families the dreadful guilt of all those sins and pernicious effects both to church and State that may ensue thereupon.'

No difference, you see, either side of the border except in the people who were winning. I quote this as a sharp reminder to any of us who are called to be apologists for the Christian church or for any Christian church in particular and to believe that history is a source for apologetic appeals and arguments. The tone of that petition, together with the tone of both mutual treatment of, and debates between, upholders of the Church of England and other Christians certainly well into the nineteenth century and occasionally today indicates how very cutting and searching is the question we have to face about the connection between the way Christians responded to and commended their faith in history and the way we ought to do so now.

Further, I deliberately focussed on the Toleration Act of 1689 and the Scots quotation of 1703 in order to bring out how, even by the beginning of the eighteenth century, we are, at least religiously only on the eve of our modern era. The attitudes expressed in the petition of 1703 and in the behaviour of High Churchmen under Queen Anne are unquestionably mediaeval. The re-establishment of the Church of England, as in the Prayer Book, Articles and Act of Uniformity of 1662, is unquestionably mediaeval. This is modified, however, by the circumstances, that a unified Christendom in both church and government has now totally and finally disappeared. Each state or realm is now behaving as the focus of human and Christian civilization, organization and identity. In the break-up of Christendom and of the visible and mono-lithic Catholic church which took place leading up to and during the Reformation and the Renaissance, men substituted the famous dictum of 'une foi, une loi, un roi' (one faith, one law, one sovereign) for the assumptions of an all-embracing imperium with an all-embracing church.

Now, it is true that this breaking-up into nation states was the transition to modernity, but the principles of both religion and statecraft which produced the godly prince and the Church of England are surely basically mediaeval, however much the actual processes moved us towards modernity. I think that it is sharply, and even shockingly, brought out in the continuing effective opposition to toleration of dissenters, to which I am drawing attention, at the beginning of the eighteenth century and which extends into the nineteenth century, if not to today. Hence appeals to history, which are alleged to be decisive for either the shaping of Christian belief or the ordering of a Christian church today have to be handled with the utmost care. The vast bulk of the formative history of the church and the churches so far lives in a world decisively different from ours. It lies also in a world which practised many evil things, in the deliberate name of the Christian religion, taking it for granted that this Christian religion was intimately related to, if not identified with, the culture and fabric of society and the ordering and maintenance of the state.

History has now deprived us of that pretension and a re-newed, if forced, study of the biblical records and of the disturbing nature both of the prophets and of Jesus have reminded us that this type of identification with all its dynamics in fact sits ill with the dynamics of the biblical stories and patterns. The wretched official Christian record on tolerance and intolerance, however much it may be understandable his-torically and culturally, may therefore serve to remind us that an appeal to history as a part of Christian apologetic has plausibility and credibility only if such an appeal is deeply critical and very self-searching. It also points us to the dangers of appealing to the past for the justification and direction of the church now, or at least to the risky ambivalence of any such appeal. Such a risky ambivalence is to be seen in the appeal of the nineteenth-century Tractarians to the past of the church, to which I will briefly turn.

However, by way of introduction to this I want to refer to something else, that is, to what may seem an absurd omission in this lecture. It is the omission of any discussion of the great Anglican divines of the second half of the sixteenth and of the seventeenth century. These include Richard Hooker, and all those writers including John Cosin (whom I must mention out of piety as Bishop of Durham), Jeremy Taylor, William Laud and many others who are cited in the compendious compilation on Anglicanism edited by P. E. More and F. L. Cross. Have I not hopelessly distorted my selective historical account by choosing to discuss political history and omitting to discuss apologetic, systematic and devotional divinity? This may be so, but I think not. I will offer some theological reflection, briefly, in the next lecture, but the point of this lecture is, I believe, sufficiently maintained with reference to the theological and devotional work of the writers referred to by pointing out that their labours were, as far as arguments and apologetics go, *ex post facto* (after the event). They were making the best case they could for the continuity of the church in the form they were receiving it or attempting to shape it. They were also doing an absolutely essential job of maintaining the pastoral, spiritual, devotional and personal life of Christian faith, in whatever circumstances, and wherever they were. That task is presumably their major contribution (especially that of many of the Caroline divines). Without the life of faith the church could not in any shape go on, and it would not be worth while that it should go on. But while their theologizing and their devotion were essential contributions to the continuing life of the Church of England and made considerable contributions to that way of life (for example, by helping it to retain more aspects and echoes of Catholic devotion and practice than

84

would otherwise have been the case), I do not believe that they made decisive contributions, either by their language or their practices, to the decisions of Crown, Parliament and bishops about the establishment and doctrine of the church.

There is a real sense in which we may say that they informed these decisions, and this is vital – indeed, as I might argue, providential. But they did not in any direct way cause or direct the decisions. Their Christian and devotional intentionality was kept alive in the church and helped to keep the church religiously alive despite all the compromises and chances of political history. But they had to react to events and make what they could of them for what they judged to be godly purposes. As a class they may well represent examples of those who make their contribution to church and to history by operating out of that providential and mysterious space, that space – the idea of which I postulated at the end of my last lecture and developed at the beginning of this one. What they did was to keep alive the gifts from the past and to keep open possibilities of the future, gifts and possibilities which were vital to the essential life of the Church of England as a living Christian organism. But this living Christian organism fitted more or less ill or more or less well into a procrustean institutional carapace worked out and modified through the vicissitudes of history. The actual form of this institution continued to become more and more anachronistic in its time and in many ways less and less suitable as the vehicle of organic Christian life and mission.

None the less it displayed a remarkable capacity for survival. As one might be inclined to argue nowadays, what keeps the Church of England going is not the Holy Spirit but the Church Commissioners. So to complete this lecture I wish to refer, inevitably briefly, to some nineteenth-century examples of this.

First, consider the events in the decade of the 1830s. In 1830 the Whigs captured Parliament from the Tories and reform was in the air. 1832 saw the passing of the Reform Act and therefore the emergence of a House of Commons well on the way to becoming the pluralistic House which it now is. If the Established Church was to develop as church in the direction of being a lively church in a pluralistic and secular nation, then its parliamentary establishment was becoming more and more anachronistic. It was also, at the time, very unpopular for the scandals and anomalies of operating. So many churchmen felt that they were seriously and dangerously threatened. On the organizational side the bishops, prompted by Bishop Blomfield of London, got Peel's Tory government of 1835 to appoint an ecclesiastical commission which Lord Melbourne's government fortunately maintained. This commission produced many reforms, got them through Parliament, and became a continuing body. The worst scandals were removed and the Church of England emerged with some sort of tolerable working system. In fact, our modern bureaucracy was on the way. Thus, as Alec Vidler remarks in his volume on the nineteenth century in the Pelican History of the Church, 'its survival as an Established Church was in practice secured, though no one could say for certain on what principle, if any, its establishment now rested.'[3] Stephen Neill, in his book on Anglicanism, is somewhat sharper: 'If the Church of England had not developed a capacity unmatched in any other Christian communion in the world for tolerating the intolerable it would have been brought to an end long ago.'[4] And so on.

This is something again, this business of the establishment and the connection with the state, which we must clearly come to in the last lecture, but my point now is that at the time an attempt was made to answer the question about the principles on which the Church of England existed. This was the famous Tractarian (or Oxford) Movement. The object of Newman, Keble and their colleagues was to recall the church, as they believed, to its apostolic title-deeds and to maintain that the Church of England depended for its existence and its calling on its standing within the apostolic succession, maintained in an unbroken continuity from the apostles through the ministry of bishops, priests and deacons. And, as Vidler comments, 'Amid all the controversies in which Anglo-Catholicism become embroiled, it gave substance once again to the great idea of the

Church of Christ as a divine society and a sacred mystery, both a home for sinners and a school for saints.'5

But our question must be: how far can the claims about history be maintained? Indeed, ought they even to be made? There can be no doubt, surely, that the Tractarians were trying to make a rather new best out of a pretty bad job. They, of course claimed that they were simply reviving the Church of England's true knowledge of its real existence and basis, a knowledge which had always been carried on unconsciously and been referred to consciously by the Laudians and the Non-Jurors. As time went on, this argument did not stand up, at least for Newman as he felt obliged to develop it, and he and some others went to Rome. Others stayed and presented the Church of England from within with an unfinished agenda about its true identity and order which we must consider in the next lecture. This unfinished agenda was reflected in the very recent debate about women and Catholic Order and so on in General Synod. But we may surely see that at least, once again, this is an *ex post facto* discovery and argument, particular theological arguments arising because of particular pressures. The pressures of the 1830s obliged the Church of England to do something. Bishop Blomfield, characteristically, as I would think, of Anglican bishops, obtained a commission. Newman and others invented or resurrected a very high theology of the history of the church and of the historical church. This revival or invention certainly made a very considerable contribution to the current life and shape of the Church of England down to this day. The value of this contribution we shall have to consider in the next lecture.

Finally, I must just squeeze in another strand in the bewildering variety of those which have emerged within and contributed to the development of the Church of England. This is the emergence, effectively during the nineteenth century, of the Anglican Communion. That is a network of churches outside the British Isles which specifically derived themselves from the Church of England. The only thing I have time to comment on is that again it clearly happened accidentally. When in

1780 the Church of England settlers in Connecticut wanted a bishop and sent one of their number to the Archbishop of Canterbury, he did not know what to do. You could have a bishop according to the rules and rights of the Church of England only with the Royal Licence and on oath of allegiance to the Crown. So for the time being the Archbishop ducked the problem and Mr Seabury was passed on to the surviving Scottish Episcopalian bishops, by whom he was duly consecrated (fortunately there were four of them and three were available so it was all canonical). This was in 1784. So the first – what? Church of England? Anglican? – bishop outside the United Kingdom returned to the United States via Scotland. As the colonies were clearly going to require bishops, an Act of 1786 followed. I cannot refrain from pointing out the nature of this act. It was passed to empower the Archbishop of Canterbury or the Archbishop of York for the time being to consecrate to the office of bishop persons being subjects, or citizens, of countries out of his Majesty's dominions. It was a Royal and Parliamentary Licence. It could only be done by Royal Licence, but it could be done without requiring them to take the oaths of allegiance and supremacy and the oath of due obedience to the Archbishop for the time being.

So, you were allowed to set up the Anglican Communion by Royal Licence, and the Royal Licence allowed you to do it outside the scope of the Royal Licence and the Archbishops of Canterbury and York. In fact, on 4 Feburary 1787 William White was consecrated Bishop of Pennsylvania and Samuel Provoost as Bishop of New York. The special significance of the occasion was marked by the participation, most unusually, of the Archbishop of York as well as the Archbishop of Canterbury. This situation allowed, in a sense, an increasing flood and series of Church of England bishops overseas. First, they were for English colonists or merchants or soldiers, but these bishoprics often developed missionary activities, though not without intense conflict at some times. I can well remember how when I was preaching in Singapore Cathedral I received a government tourist leaflet which referred to the way in which this church had been built by Bishop Heber (who is much remembered for his hymns and his missionary work) 'with the labour of convicts', because in fact Bishop Heber got the church built through the civil government and by using convicts. So the very Anglican cathedral of Singapore perfectly expresses the ambiguity and the accidental and confusing nature of this development.

By 1867 there were in fact 108 bishops, most of them overseas, to be invited to the Lambeth Conference, and 76 of them came. By 1968, 459 came, and by 1988 there are so many to come that all sorts of them are being left out and people are having to work out on what basis they should come. Typical of the confusion we are in – or the opportunity we have. For what do we have here? Nobody knows, though it has certainly happened.

Therefore, I suggest that among the agenda items to be considered we have to include the following. What is the significance of the unfinished theological agenda which the Church of England has from its separate and separated emergence in the time of Henry VIII? At that time it was to do with Lutherans and Calvinists and so on, but it has now come to be to do with Protestants and Catholics. Is the Church of England creatively comprehensive or irremediably confused? Secondly, how can and should the Church of England face up to and live with, and for the future deal with, its entanglement with the state? What sort of anachronism am I? A scandal or a useful one? Thirdly (and I have to slip this in), what is the significance of the parochial inheritance and coverage from the past which is more or less maintained at the present, although very often more in appearance than in practice? Fourthly, what on earth is the Anglican Communion?

# 4

## *The Future of Anglicanism*

In following up this invitation to be the Hensley Henson lecturer to consider the appeal to history as an integral part of Christian apologetics, I have been looking into that history which has produced the Church of England as it at present exists. I have been doing this partly as a way of pursuing more general theological questions about the interaction between the accidents of history and the providence of God. But I have been pursuing these more general questions in order to see how the way in which we could reasonably and properly – perhaps probably – answer questions about God and history would throw light on, or be relevant to, the decisions which the Church of England, in relationship with the Anglican Communion, ought to take; questions which are at present pressing upon it or pressing within it.

So I come now to my concluding lecture about the future of Anglicanism. One thing is certain: all will not be revealed in it! But let me begin by summarizing my arguments which have led me to a certain point in offering an answer to the question, 'What *is* the Church of England?' I suggest that a historically correct descriptive answer would be something like this. The Church of England is the institutional result in England of the left-over effects and the knock-on effects of the activities of a line of so-called godly princes from Henry VIII to Charles II, operating with the help of Parliament and of such divines as would assist them, on the late mediaeval form of the Christian catholic church of the West which the first of them (Henry VIII) found in England when he came to the throne.

The Church of England did not, of course, emerge from the loins of Henry VIII; it is much more complicated than that. But I do not think that Anglo-Catholics can get away with treating Henry VIII as a smoke-screen either. He is undoubtedly one of the supervening causes. This Church of England has given rise, in the last two hundred years, to what are now a set of autonomously organized churches scattered across the world but in some way grouped together in what is called the Anglican Communion. The question to which this concluding lecture is addressed is: What are we to make of this? Where 'we' are the class of persons defined as follows.

First, the persons who share the belief that the God who is reflected through and in the stories and patterns and prayers of the Bible is truly God. Secondly, the set of persons who, along with that, believe that Jesus and the things about him are powerfully decisive clues about who this God is, about how he interacts and transacts with men and women in the world. Thirdly (we now come to a much more narrowing definition which will cut down the class which will fit into the first definitions), people who hold that the Church of England is the way through which we have received our faith and our calling so that the Church of England has to be understood as in some way or other being within the providence of God. Now I realize that this third defining characteristic both takes some believing and also somewhat restricts the class of persons to whom it applies, including those in the class of the Christian. However, I hope to show before I have finished this lecture what I believe to be the ecumenical role of the Church of England and of the Anglican communion.

In order to make something of the history of the Church of England and of its present state of affairs, what do we (as defined above) have at our disposal? As I have been arguing throughout these lectures, we have a set of stories, patterns and prayers collected together in the Bible and made use of in a dynamic, continuing way in the actual and concrete living of the church, the churches and groups and groupings of Christians (I might add, and gropings of Christians!) from the first century after Christ to today, and with an increasingly wide geographical dissemination as well as historical distribution. These stories and patterns and prayers are focussed, according to the things about Jesus – as presented at any rate in the first three of the Gospels – by being about the kingdom of God. We may compare what Christians call the Lord's Prayer. The kingdom of God is the focussing symbol of a faith and claim that the life of men and women and the history of humankind can be made sense of within a story because the universe itself is part of that story. This story is the story of God's risking creation so that he may share love in the establishing of a kingdom, a city, a promised land or a shared and shareable space, with persons or beings who are capable of relationships with him and yet are other than himself.

To be a Christian is to be caught up in this story and to be made a part of those consciously concerned with the coming-true of the story, with the twist of the direction given to the story by the discovery and conviction that Jesus is the Christ. To discover that Jesus (that is, the particular man of Nazareth, Son of Mary, and so on, and so on) is the Christ (which is what, for Christians, the resurrection is all about) is to discover that in enabling the story, in taking part in the story, and in steadfastly contributing to making the story come true, God pursues ways of immanence, identification, service and suffering which are a severe affront to the normal, or indeed normative, human ideas of power. In addition, these are a deep disturbance to what most people expect, or seem to be able consistently to cope with, about the role and function of religion. Thus, as is already clear within what Christians call the Old Testament, the very organisms and institutions which emerged for special roles within the story, which are the recipients of formative contributions to the story and are called to live by that story, to witness to that story among the nations and to play various roles in exploring and developing the story, often become at odds with the story and can become obstacles to its development and contradictions to its whole ethos, hope and direction.

A type-specimen example of a providential and prophetic intervention within the story and the development of the story, and within the goings-on of history, and indeed as a response to and contribution to the goings-on of history, is to be read from the book of the prophet Micah: 'Hear, O mountains, the Lord's accusation! Listen, you everlasting foundations of the earth, for the Lord has a case against his people. He is lodging a charge against Israel' (6.2). This is the translation in what is called the New International Version of the Bible; the Authorized Version puts it rather splendidly that the Lord has a controversy with his people. To receive, discover or respond to a providential part in the story is not to receive any guarantee of good behaviour, or assured standing. It is to become a conscious part of the community of communities who are co-opted into, or emerge out of, the story. These chosen people have a call, a responsibility and an opportunity to collaborate with God and with one another in discovering the development of the story – shaping that development and being shaped by that development under the faith and with the practice that the story is not made up by us alone but is a dialogue and a development with a tripartite dynamism. The three vectors of the dynamics come from God, from women and men in a developing awareness of and response to God (a developing response which requires continual practice and continual correction); and thirdly, the goings-on which are the subject of history and of science.

Thus, the story of the kingdom is a claim that reality can be responded to and be made sense of on the understanding and practice that men and women who are in the image of God are engaged, or can be engaged, through the stuff of history and science, in a communications system with God which can and does give direction to a divine and human project which is of lasting significance and promise. Man is not – to pick up a phrase of Sartre's – 'a useless passion'. Men and women are, or

93

can be, on their way to that kingdom of God to which they themselves have a contribution to make.

The Christian story is thus not basically and definitively a religious story. In its basic insight and in its authentic movement it is a story about the whole of the universe and the possibilities of personal beings, including men and women, who emerge within that universe in relation to that divine possibility, presence and promise who is encountered or glimpsed as the God of the universe. From the Old Testament onwards it is made clear (within the Old Testament itself it is made clear) that whatever necessary part the Isrealites and their religion have to play in the providence and purposes of God, their actual religious performances and practices are at least as likely to be an obstacle to, or an affront to, or a misrepresentation of, the divine direction and development of the story as a contribution to it. Similarly, a principal role in the rejection of Jesus which actually and providentially, as we might say, contributed to the decisive turn in the story brought about by the things concerning Jesus, was played by the religious people and the religious leaders of his time. Further, Christian religious leaders have used that role of the Jews, as portrayed in the formative stories of the New Testament, to add to a disastrous and disgraceful antisemitism, an antisemitism contributed to with great enthusiasm at various points and places in history by Christian mobs and Christian rulers and Christian religious leaders.

Thus it is quite clear that there are no authentic grounds derivable from the story to support any claim or guarantee that Christian religious institutions (that is to say, the church or the churches) are preserved from being ungodly, or obstacles to and contradictions of the divine and human story which gives them their title deeds and to which they are called to contribute. Moreover, history makes it clear again and again that the church and the churches do indeed betray, distort and wellnigh deny the story. Certainly they frequently render it highly implausible and incredible. Hence, as I believe, the theological and practical importance, as a sort of symbol, of my rather

94

clumsily mixed metaphor, produced in my previous lecture, about the Caroline divines making a vital contribution to the essential life of the Church of England as a living Christian organism, fitting more or less ill, or more or less well, into a procrustean institutional carapace, worked out and modified through the vicissitudes of history. (How history could actually work out a lobster's shell I am not clear. Hence the muddle and the mixture of the metaphor. I simply thought of it and I rather like it!)

The church and the churches have a necessary part to play in the story, but the story is the story of the kingdom, not of the church. Church and kingdom are interrelated in ways which are subject to the vicissitudes and accidents of history, including the inadequate and sinful distortions of men and women in power and out of power, and the church and the churches are as much required to submit to, and be changed by, discoveries and criticisms as the story develops, as they also have the opportunity to proclaim the possibilities of the story and share in the positive developments of the story. The church is certainly not in charge of the story and cannot, mercifully, even control it.

I cannot now develop further this narrative approach to faith, theology and tradition. Nor can I pursue the implications of this for issues of epistemology and of value in general. I am clear that they are there, and I believe that they are very pertinent to philosophy of science as well as to theology and, more especially, to the wrestling and rethinking that we are urgently required to do about the whole matter of how we sustain and pursue truly human and realistically hopeful purposes and ends in the face of the problems pressed upon us by our current scientific, technological, political and social developments and dilemmas. I find some very helpful and suggestive argumentation about this in the book of Alasdair MacIntyre's to which I have already referred, *After Virtue*.

Now, however, I must concentrate on relating the approach I have sketched out to the questions which are pressing about the future of the Anglican church. To do this I propose to draw briefly on some points made by MacIntyre about what he calls a tradition in relation to a narrative approach to the understanding of human life and the virtues and possibilities of it. I will take this up from a point which I have already made and which is central to my argument about the interaction between accident and providence. That is, that within a narrative understanding of goings on, purpose and unpredictability go together. Thus, in *After Virtue* Alasdair MacIntyre makes the following observation (he has just been discussing Karl Marx and *The Eighteenth Brumaire of Louis Bonaparte*): 'I call Marx's account less than satisfactory partly because he wishes to present the narrative of human social life in a way that will be compatible with a view of the life as law-governed and predictable in a particular way.'[1] I am challenging the view of the life of the church as law-governed and predictable in a particular way. Hence my interest in what follows. 'But it is crucial that at any given point in an enacted dramatic narrative we do not know what will happen next... This unpredictability coexists with a second crucial characteristic of all lived narratives, a certain teleological character. We live out our lives, both individually and in our relationships with one another, in the light of certain conceptions of a possible shared future.'[2] That, to my mind, would be a very good one-sentence description of Christians 'living their lives in certain conceptions of a possible shared future', a possible shared future being the kingdom of God.

He then goes on:

> Unpredictability and teleology therefore coexist as part of our lives; like characters in a fictional narrative we do not know what will happen next but nonetheless our lives have a certain form which projects itself towards our future. Thus the narratives which we live out have both an unpredictable and a partly teleological character. If the narrative of our individual and social lives is to continue intelligibly – and either type of narrative may lapse into unintelligibility – it is always both the case that there are constraints on how the

story can continue *and* that within those constraints there are indefinitely many ways that it can continue. A central thesis begins to emerge: man is in his actions and practice, as well as in his fictions, essentially a story-telling animal. He is not essentially, but becomes through his history, a teller of stories that aspire to truth.' – [A teller of stories that aspire to truth. I am not, as the major-general in the Pirates of Penzance might be saying 'telling a terrible story'; it is a story that aspires to truth.] – But the key question for men is not about their own authorship. I can only answer the question 'What am I to do?' if I can answer the prior question 'Of what story or stories do I find myself a part?'[3]

Note three things about that. Of what story do I find myself part? The church is both the product and the purveyor of a particular claim and answer to that question, including the claim that the story the church is called to be part of is potentially universal and all-embracing because it is a divine story. Secondly, note what I believe the systems analysis and organizational and systematic people call 'equifiniality'. The reference that if the narrative of our individual and social life is to continue intelligibly, it is always both the case that there are constraints on how the story can continue – so various lines, or paths or forces and so on are closed by the current constraint – and that within these constraints there are indefinitely many ways that it can continue. The possibility is of a system reaching a visualized end by a whole different series of possibilities and if one set of possibilities gets blocked, another set of possibilities is opened, so that you may have equifiniality – there are more ways than one of getting to the same end (and possibly an infinite number of ways, certainly a very great number of ways). This goes with constraints and risks. For example, if I may illustrate, the blessed phrase TINA – there is no alternative – is not true either politically or ecclesiastically. Sometimes it becomes necessary to consider what I have come to call TMBAW – there must be another way. That applies, again, both ecclesiastically as well as politically. Sometimes there are a variety of independent and interacting ways which are equally or indifferently desirable, risky or share limitations but differing limitations.

This point I take to be of central importance with regard to the Church of England, the future of Anglicanism and ecumenism. I shall come to that later. The drift of the argument is that history shows, and theology would support and practice require, that there should be a variety of ways of expressing attempts to be the church and to serve the kingdom. Thirdly, the whole point which Alasdair MacIntyre makes about projecting ourselves towards our future. Thus, with regard to theology and the church, I want to draw attention to something which in my own jargon I call the eschatological transposition. A story moves towards its end. 'Jesus is the Messiah' means, among other things, that he is the end or the bringer of that end to which God calls and will bring things. Hence, for instance, the expression 'alpha and omega'. The Christian version of the divine human-narrative and of the purpose of the divine-human interactions and transactions is concerned with the movement towards the end. Backward-looking appeals to the past, especially a claim to tradition as something formed by, and deposited in, the past, are – as we have often been reminded, but now as we are surely more sharply reminded than ever – fundamentally vicious in theological principle, not in the sense of Christian appeals to gifts received from the past which can now be used in the present for moving towards the end and the future, but in the sense of relying on gifts and definitions deposited in the past and fixed by the past. The eschatological transposition is vital, and it is forced upon us both by the theological dynamics of the biblical and Christian narrative and also by any appeal to history as an integral part of Christian apologetic. For such an appeal shows, I believe because of what I have been investigating with regard to the emergence of the Church of England, that *history has destroyed our right to, or a possibility of, a definitive appeal to the past*.

First, we have the problem of the break wherever you may

recognize it (although, of course, history is a continuum), the break that I, for the moment, decided to locate somewhere round about 1705 as I was hoping that that was a fairly insignificant date: say the break of the eighteenth century, wherever it is. The story itself requires us to live in the world at large for the sake of the universal story at large. It is a contradiction of the story to construct a religious ghetto called the church which claims the right to its own totally privileged epistemology independently of whatever goes on. The church has a right and a duty to press, pursue, work out and see what develops in practice by its own presentation and pursuit of, and commitment to, the story. But there must be an interaction with all the other goings-on where God also is.

Secondly, a simple definitive appeal to the past is also ruled out (and I have made this point, really, several times) by the evils revealed by any apologetic investigation of the past. In my last lecture I used the intolerance of toleration. I have referred in this lecture to Christian antisemitism. There is alarmingly much more. The church and the Christian tradition are in practice far too immoral to have any definite claims defined by past deposits alone.

Thirdly, in any case this appeal to the past is so implausible on inspection. It keeps on coming up – we got it only the other day: the Vincentian canon again, 'What is always, what is everywhere and what is by all'. That only works when you choose which bits of always and which bits of everywhere and which bits by all you are going to pay attention to. That seems to me to be so simply obvious that I cannot understand why, except for sociologial, psychological and power reasons, anyone ever refers to it. It seems to me quite simply obvious and I have no respect for people who use that argument on its own – they are just not looking at the facts. We need, of course, to be critical of the spirit of this age. Relevance, which I shall come to, is a very dangerous criterion; but we need plainly, and with equal necessity, to be critical of the spirit of past ages. However much store we may set by the stories, patterns and prayers of the Bible, and however much we may recognize and experience the necessity of getting on to the stories by belonging to a community which is part of the community of communities living by and from the Christian story, surely we can no longer escape the overwhelming evidence for, and experience of, relativization. I personally am convinced that in and through the stories which are enshrined in the Bible and in and through the communities which live as the church we authentically receive the invitation to respond to, work with and receive from the Absolute, the Absolute who is God. But this is always received in the relative, the provisional, the uncertain and the changing. Both the Bible and the church, I believe, are divine gifts. But they have emerged as all other divine gifts in history, deeply shaped and even scarred by history, and they depend for their effectiveness (like all divine gifts) on divine action now and human response now. It occured to me when preparing these lectures (and I offer this as one of my hostages to fortune) that one ought to say 'revelation is always now, or never'.

Therefore what I am struggling to formulate might provisionally be described as a relativized positivism. A relativized positivism of both Bible and church related to, and preserved in, a tradition operated by a community of communities for living the story in the present and moving with the story into the future. Here I return to Alasdair MacIntyre in order to illustrate how it seems to me that we must finally break out of the notion of tradition as giving us things and directions from the past which, being fixed, either serve as dead weights to stop us giving the story liveliness and grip in the present, or serve as some sort of school prize which makes us and our church one-up and superior (whatever the pressures of the present or demands and possibilities of the future). The practical implications of this are, I believe, well pointed to in a further set of quotations I want to take from MacIntyre.

First,

We are apt to be misled here – [that is, in the discussion of tradition] – by the ideological uses to which the concept of tradition has been put by conservative political theorists.

100

Characteristically such theorists have followed Burke in contrasting tradition with reason and the stability of tradition with conflict.

That is very important and very much *ad rem*. I, for instance, am always accused of being a rationalist and not a traditionalist; also, everyone wants to dodge conflict in order to be traditional. As MacIntyre rightly says:

> Both contrasts obfuscate. For all reasoning takes place within the context of some traditional mode of thought, transcending through criticism and invention the limitations of what had hitherto been reasoned in that tradition; this is as true of modern physics as of mediaeval logic.

And now a very important point.

> Moreover, when a tradition is in good order it is always partially constituted by an argument about the goods the pursuit of which gives to that tradition its particular point and purpose. So when an institution ... is the bearer of a tradition of practice or practices, its common life will be partly, but in a centrally important way, constituted by a continuous argument as to what it in fact is or ought to be and what being a good example of it is. Traditions when vital embody continuities of conflict. Indeed, when a tradition becomes Burkean, it is always dying or dead.

And I can assure you that in the recent debate in General Synod there was a smell of death. Elderly gentlemen, largely, from within a decaying institution, discussing questions which had very little resonance with the sufferings and the realities and the challenges and the promises of what was going on outside.

> A living tradition then is an historically expended, socially embodied, argument, and an argument precisely in part about the goods which constitute that tradition... To recognize this is, of course, also to recognize the existence of an additional virtue, one whose importance is perhaps most

101

obvious when it is least present, the virtue of having an adequate sense of the traditions to which one belongs or which confront one. The virtue is not to be confused with any form of conservative antiquarianism. I am not praising those who choose the conventional conservative role of *laudator temporis acti*. It is rather the case that an adequate sense of tradition manifests itself in a grasp of those future possibilities which the past has made available to the present.[4]

To use this in relation to what I have nicknamed the eschatological transposition required by the Christian narrative and story, I would add that the future possibilities which the past has made available to the present have to be sought for and discerned under the pressures of a tripartite dynamism similar to that to which I have already referred. There is the presence of God in mystery, in prayer, in worship and in the personal experiences of faith and commitment which keep people (even despite themselves, sometimes) as pilgrims and pursuers within the story. There is the pressure of men and women in their experience, needs and joys and confusions and distortions, and there is the pressure of what is going on and the problems this creates for the story and for the living of men and women. Discernment is a difficult matter, always provisional and necessarily requiring mutual accountability between those who hold that they are called into the story and have a responsibility for developing the story. For instance, as I have just mentioned, relevance is a tricky matter. Relevance, I believe, is always a proper question but never a defining answer on its own. Similarly, tradition is always a proper question but never a defining answer on its own. The felt needs of, or the state of acceptability of, something to women and men are always proper questions but never defining answers on their own. The story is far more searching and far more extensive than any of these things and there is always, also, the authentic scandal of Jesus and the kingdom.

So the people of the story need one another in their different perspectives, practices, understandings and misunderstandings under God and in God and in response to the pressures and opportunities of men and women and the goings-on in the world, if we are to be authentic receivers of the story and godly contributors to it.

Consider, therefore, by way perhaps of further exploration and exemplification, the bearing of this theoretical and practical approach on the sort of questions that I have raised about the future of Anglicanism. First, I believe it makes clear that we must free ourselves from what has been more or less (although only very approximately) the past historical reality of a great church. This has now become a historical illusion and it is increasingly of no use in its currently maintained form for the immediate or medium-term future. The monolithic and hierarchical one and undivided catholic church of the Mediterranean oecoumene (inhabited civilized world) which, we might say, nearly existed for a considerable number of what we call Christian centuries is gone. We cannot have it back and we should not want it back, nor in fact do we need it back. Hence the giving of definitive weight (as distinct from giving very serious, continuing and maintained conversation and attention) to the Roman Catholic Church and the Orthodox Churches in decisions as to the form and ordering of the church, or as to the identity of the church, or as to the explorations and experiments of the church is, I am persuaded, an historical illusion, a theological misreading and an unproductive practical error. The question we have to face is how we now make a responsible use of the gifts God has allowed us to receive through the accidents of history and the providences of personal discipleship in our versions of the story, the traditions and the church. How do we make use of these to contribute to moving forwards towards a better and a more effective service of the kingdom of God and a new, wider and more effectively articulated expression of the Catholicity of God? The church of God is not to be identified with any existing institution, and the churches are called to contribute by mutual conversation and provocation, particular repentances and general reformation to the continuing formation of God's church in relation to the development of the story of the kingdom. Christendom has to be left definitively behind, so that we may move through a mutually responsible and currently interactive pluralism to new forms of catholicism which clearly and plainly relate the Christian institution which bears the story of the kingdom to the needs of the whole world for movements towards unity and love.

In practice this requires something like a federal model of the church in relation to the story of the kingdom and in relation to the needs, pressures and opportunities of the whole world and of its goings on. The model of a monolithic, Christian, Catholic church which would gradually extend its empire over the whole world in the name of and as an expression of the kingdom is clearly rendered obsolescent by history. These historical pressures force us to look again at the dynamics and directions of the story of the kingdom and the nature of the God who is both the author and the hoped-for finisher of the story. In the light of what has happened and in the light of things concerning Jesus and of the symbol of the Trinity which insists that Jesus is God in the one and only sense in which God is God (the Greek for that is *homoousios*) we are now called to see that the imperial model of the church, its existence and its mission which implied a monolithic and powerful church gradually conquering the world for the kingdom is in fact, in theory and in desirability a false and misleading model, whatever dynamic purpose it has served in the past. God is not an imperial controller and triumphalistic manager. He is a persevering artist, a suffering servant and an indefatigable and invincible love.

Hence the monolithic church, the triumphalistic church and the carrying-all-before-it church is out. It has been falsified by history and is seen to be false theologically in the light of history, but consistently with the story. As with everything, however, from the human point of view in both the processes of science and in the events of history, things have only become clear about what is falsified and about what must be cast aside. We cannot therefore be clear about what is verified, and about what will continue to make its way through history, under the providence of God, until the end. So we cannot have a clear and certain blueprint of how to pattern the church now and in the future. All that we can do – and surely this is quite sufficient – is to be reasonably and practically clear about the gifts we have received in the course of living into and out of the story, and how we may now use them for the ongoing pursuit of, and contribution to, the story.

These gifts include the Bible as an essential reference point for, and renewing source of, the stories, patterns and prayers which give the story existence, direction and continuation. They include also those crystallizations of tradition and traditions so far which include both the early classical creeds and definitions and also some contributions from later confessions. Dogmas, however, are to be received as gifts and reference points for provocation, reinterpretation and signposting. Dogmas are not inerrant descriptions of divine mysteries from which may be deduced inerrant prescriptions about the pattern of God, the ordering of the church or the ethics of Christian living. God is not to be mapped. History is not to be predicted. Living in the story of the kingdom cannot set us free from decisions – not only about whether we shall obey, but also about how and what it is to obey.

Thirdly, along with the Bible and the deposit of tradition there is the trinitarian worship of the community of communities who contribute to both the existence of and the expression and exploration of the church. This worship is an identifying part of the church and a dynamic contribution to the ongoing life of the church, for two reasons. First, because it is focussed in the challenging and directing dynamism of the symbol of the Trinity with its interacting concepts of transcendence, particularity and immanence. Secondly, because a necessary part of the ongoing life of the story and the faith communities of the story is that in and through them people commit their central insights and hopes to what they believe is and will be centrally worth while (as St Augustine said, 'Where do you direct your love?'). So along with Bible and tradition

105

go the demands, offers and experiences of trinitarian worship. Further, all this has actually to be held together in structured and structuring communities. Hence a proper concern within the story and in terms of the story for the ordering of the church and of the interrelationship between churches. But this concern has to be worked out dynamically, pragmatically, provisionally and experimentally. What is required is a responsible and critical concern for ordering, in relation to the story, in relation to realistic history and in relation to current demand. What is not required is a triumphalistic and unrealistic demand that one pattern or ordering understood according to one particular intention must be determinative of the future church or a condition of intercommunion and mutual recognition between present churches. Such a demand is inconsistent with the whole pattern and dynamic of the story of the kingdom, is rendered highly implausible by the actual failures (whatever also are the real achievements) of all churches, whatever their ordering, and is rendered offensive by the overwhelming evidence that the fruit of the Spirit is not in any sort of correlation with the particular ordering of particular churches.

Finally, along with Bible, tradition, trinitarian worship and a concern for responsible ordering of the church and interrelationships between churches must go a determined commitment to mutual accountability, mutual provocation and mutual collaboration between us in as wide as possible a group of those communities who believe themselves to be communities of the story of faith. Along these lines I believe we should arrive at a picture of any contemporary expression of the church as that which can be picked up in and through a network of networks, which have emerged in and through history and are marked, more or less, by a commitment to and a concern with the five identifying marks or interactive sources of dynamism which I have briefly indicated. Some such approach should set both the Church of England and the Anglican Communion free to be totally realistic about the historical accidents and actual errors in the process which has produced them so far and also to be quite sufficiently clear about our actual, current identity and the gifts and opportunities which we have received from God and which we are now required to work out in sharing with other churches the work of the kingdom in the world. A dynamic model of a network of networks which I am working towards here suggests the following clues, which I will list quickly just as examples with reference to the questions and problems of the Church of England and Anglicanism which I have touched upon in these lectures.

First, the Church of England, along with and in interaction with the rest of the Anglican Communion, would do well to regard its unfinished theological agenda as on the whole a blessing rather than a curse, however difficult it may prove at times and in practice to handle. I mean the unfinished agenda about the nature and identity of the church and its theology. In Henry VIII's and Queen Elizabeth I's day, Lutheranism and Calvinism; then as it moved on, the nature and status of episcopacy. I mean the unfinished theological agenda about the nature and relationship of Catholicism and Protestantism. These are not to be sorted out and solved by taking them in their old terms and with material from their past. They are, in their current forms and in forward-looking terms, precisely part of the material for – and much of the provocation for – working out the function of the network of churches for current tasks and into the future. Moreover, it is essential to be clear about the point I took from MacIntyre's formulation that conflict about the actual direction and goods and goals of a tradition is precisely the sign of a living tradition. Any forward shaping of the church must make space for, and provide for, dynamic living out of conversation and conflicts, which test out the current version or versions of the story as they develop.

Secondly, the Church of England has a peculiarly sharp problem at the moment about its relationship to the state in England and to the nation in England. There are, of course, other churches of other traditions in other countries which have their own versions of this problem or the aftermath of this problem. It is essential to work out ways of advancing on this which eventually set the Church of England free from its current bondage to a wholly outmoded picture of the church as the religious side of a Christian state which in itself is a standing-in for Christendom. However, this disentangling from what might be called the left-overs of history needs, if possible, to be done while making the best use of what can still be seen as current gifts and opportunities from history. For example, can we find a way (I am not at all sure we can, but I think it is a proper question) by working with our ecumenical fellow-Christians in this country and by learning from our fellow Anglicans in other countries, of transposing the remains of folk religion, other vestiges of a desire for a Christian nation, and the remaining opportunities of a parochial system which still theoretically covers every area of the land into the shape of an ecumenical church which, while it can no longer pretend to be a national church (still less a state church) can nonetheless know and show that it stands, and can be seen to stand (even as a Christian minority) for the universal concern of the universal God of the whole of humankind and therefore for every citizen of a particular nation, whatever his or her class, creed, sex or other differentiating characteristic? Certainly no positive way forward will be found on this very difficult road unless and until we free ourselves from regressive and unrealistic nostalgia about being the state church established in and for a Christian nation. History has disproved and dismantled this, and Christian eschatology demands that believing and committed Christians work away from this and move beyond this.

A sub-heading in this problem area is the need of the Church of England to work out a clear and independent style of self-government for itself. Here is an item for the agenda. At the moment we are almost hopelessly confused in a nearly inextricable mix of old hierarchy, old parliamentarianism and newish synodism which already seems to be getting tired and old. Sometimes one feels one has the worst of all possible worlds – but that, of course is a faithless response. The Church of England has doubtless survived at least equally bad muddles, though I doubt it has survived worse ones.

Here the Church of England has much to learn from its colleagues in the Anglican Communion who have had to work out their own ways of self-identity and self-government in relation to the accidents of their history, their understanding of the Christian story through an Anglican form and their existence as minorities in a nation and a state which is either non-Christian or certainly not Anglican.

Finally, I must draw the briefest attention to the opportunities which are open to the Church of England in, and in connection with, what is genuinely a world-wide Anglican Communion. The opportunities which are thereby given to operate with confidence but with humility as a network which, while it has its own identity, does not and cannot have triumphalist, monopolistic or imperialistic identity. Therefore along with its unfinished theological agenda and its many historical loose ends the Church of England, in the context of the Anglican Communion, is particularly fitted to link up with and work with many other Christian networks and churches across the whole spectrum which is occupied by that diverse community of communities which presents and represents the Christian church across the world today. In one area there are the links with the Roman Catholic and the Orthodox; in another there are links with Lutheranism and the Reformed, and in yet another with, say, the charismatics and independents and so on. At least I would think that an appeal to history would serve to show that the Church of England, as a committed and interdependent member of the Anglican Communion, has as much to be thankful for for being itself and as many accidental but providential opportunities for serving the kingdom as it has ever had, but only if and as it is ready to go forward and does not try to settle what is its identity from the past and then try to enforce that. Such a way lies open to obsolescence, mere sectarianism and a retreat into an egocentric cult of those who like their religion to be familiar, cosy and a protection from reality.

The story, the providence and the dynamic of the kingdom of God, in the name of God, Father, Son and Holy Spirit, is something very different from such backward looking. It is something much more exciting, and something that can be much more promising, as well as much more costly.

What is the future of the Anglican Communion? It depends, under God, on what we make it, and how we have the courage and insight to negotiate it.

# Notes

*Part One*

Chapter 2   *God and the Theologian*

1. H. A. Hodges, *God beyond Knowledge*, Macmillan 1979, p. 9.

2. Augustine, *De Civitate Dei* XXII, 30.

*Part Two*

Chapter 1   *What is Church History?*

1. R. V. Sellers, *The Council of Chalcedon. A Historical and Doctrinal Survey*, SPCK 1953, pp. 96f.

2. Aloys Grillmeier, *Christ in Christian Tradition*, second edition, Mowbrays 1975, p. 529.

3. Karl Popper, *The Poverty of Historicism*, Routledge and Kegan Paul 1957, paperback edition 1986, pp. 133f.

Chapter 2   *Historicism and Acts of God*

1. Alasdair MacIntyre, *After Virtue*, second (corrected) edition, Duckworth 1985, p. 221.

Chapter 3   *The Emergence of Anglicanism*

1. Owen Chadwick, *The Reformation*, The Pelican History of the Church, Volume 3, Penguin Books 1964, revised 1969 and 1972, p. 97.

2. Ibid., p. 211.

3. Alec Vidler, *The Church in an Age of Revolution*, The Pelican History of the Church, Volume 5, Penguin Books 1962, revised 1972 and 1974, p. 48.

4. Stephen Neill, *Anglicanism*, Penguin Books 1958, reprinted Mowbrays 1977, p. 254.

5. Vidler, op. cit., p. 54.

Chapter 4   *The Future of Anglicanism*
1. Alasdair MacIntyre, *After Virtue*, p. 215.
2. Ibid.
3. Ibid., p .216.
4. Ibid., pp. 221f., 223.